Flowing with the Go

A Jiu-Jitsu Journey of the Soul

By
Elena Stowell

Published in the United States by BQB Publishing
(Boutique of Quality Books Publishing Company)
www.bqbpublishing.com

Printed in the United States of America

ISBN 978-1-937084-62-2 (p)
ISBN 978-1-937084-63-9 (e)
ISBN 978-1-937084-80-6 (p - Brazilian Portuguese)
ISBN 978-1-937084-81-3 (e - Brazilian Portuguese)

Library of Congress Control Number: 2012938490

Book design by Robin Krauss, www.lindendesign.biz
Cover illustration by Leah Jennings
Back cover photo by Holly Holman

To my heart, Carly,
who continues to inspire the world,
here on earth and there in heaven.

Mom

A portion of proceeds from this book will go to the
Carly Stowell Foundation
for Education in Athletic and Music Performance

"The mission of the Carly Stowell Foundation is to provide enhanced education in athletics and music to young people who demonstrate passion for learning and a commitment to excel.

"We support individualized instruction and group activities that include teams and ensembles, develop potential and leadership, teach responsibility, and foster creativity and expression."

www.carlystowellfoundation.org

Do what you love, love what you do.

Preface

T his manuscript is rooted in a mother's love for her daughter and what happens to that mother when the daughter is gone. Four and a half years ago, my daughter Carly passed away suddenly, before my eyes. And that is where this journey begins.

In many ways, this is a story about grief, but it also is a story of resiliency, self-discovery, and the healing power of belonging.

Carly and I shared a great deal of time together—supporting her basketball career and musical pursuits, molding her dreams, and, well, everything that goes along with having a teenage daughter. After she was gone, I didn't find joy in basketball, in hopes and dreams, or in me.

So it was a surprise to many people—and no one more than me—that I found joy in a sport that previously I knew nothing about: Jiu-Jitsu.

Jiu-Jitsu is a martial art that practices the grappling aspect of hand-to-hand combat. It was both physically and mentally challenging. I found muscles I never knew I had, and I found out that many of the spiritual tenets that underpin Jiu-Jitsu provided just the right spiritual guidance I needed to work through my grief. I also found a gym that was filled with people who accepted me "as is" and never gave up on me, even when I gave up on myself.

In this story, I introduce the people who made an impact on my journey: my coach James Foster, who is the owner of the gym and a second-degree black belt, my other coaches at the gym, my friends, my doctors, my family. Through the sparring sessions that became a part of my journey—both in and out of the gym—I have been able to piece together what I hope to be a map of my traveled path and promise for the future. The antics herein are at times garnished with my sophomoric sense of humor and, at other times, with an immense depth of frustration and sorrow.

Working out is so similar to working through grief. In my manuscript, I share openly and honestly my emotional rollercoaster. Tied into that rollercoaster are the contributions of my grief therapist and my naturopath, without whom I could not have found a way to move forward when the obstacles seemed insurmountable. It is my hope that my readers will find inspiration in these words and find comfort that they are not alone with their own feelings of loss.

My tale concludes with my training for and participating in the World Championships—and getting back into the GO of life—hence, *Flowing with the Go*. Sometimes the key to survival and renewal is found in the most unlikely of places.

—Elena

Foreword

*T*he first day Elena stepped into my school, I had no knowledge of the tragedy that had fractured her life—a horrible event which in a roundabout way led her to seek out training in martial arts and, through apparently random events, to my school. My first meeting with Elena showed me a person who, like most students who are new to the mats, needed direction and guidance. I had no idea how much, until my assistant coach and close friend Rick (or Brick as you will come to know him) informed me of the tragedy Elena had recently endured.

Elena didn't know that I knew, not for a long time; in fact, it was she who would finally come to me with her sorrowful tale. And even though it was not common knowledge between us at first, I always kept her situation at the forefront of my instructing Elena. Every word that I chose, the way it was spoken, and the manner in which I instructed her was tempered by my knowledge of her tragedy and what I felt was the best approach to help her become whole again. In my heart, I knew that she could live again and that the art of Brazilian Jiu-Jitsu would be a major factor in her rebirth.

I've been humbled and honored to have witnessed Elena's transformation and strength. I am proud of her, her dedication, her hard work. To have played a small role in helping her persevere and accomplish many of her goals, I am also transformed. To see her smiling, to witness her joy of life again, is a gift for all of us who know her.

Elena, you are a true inspiration to me, and I look forward to the day that I promote you to the rank of black belt in Brazilian Jiu-Jitsu. You have only scratched the surface of your true potential. Remember: "A Black Belt is a White Belt who never quit"!

With Love,

James Foster
Owner and Head Coach
Foster Brazilian Jiu-Jitsu

It's Okay To Cry . . .

*M*artial arts training benefits the body, the mind, the soul, without a doubt. But there is something even deeper about the sport . . . it draws kindred spirits.

As a coach and reverent student of the sport, I firmly believe the art form draws in and captures people who need to be there, as it did with Elena.

Many times, the whole experience is like walking in the right door at the right time and meeting the right person at the perfect moment.

When I first met Elena, I remember most vividly wanting to stop her tears, to erase her fears, to help her heal. We all did. I believe that's why she was sent to Foster's, a life-changing moment guised as an apparent random act through an Internet search.

Perhaps for Elena, the darkness will never fully go away, the wound will never fully heal, and the pain found within her heart and soul will always be there!

But through Jiu-Jitsu and her teammates and coaches, her spirit is certainly fortified anew, her mind has learned to handle the emotions, and her body is strong. She has regained control of Elena.

And she also has learned this important life lesson: "It's okay to cry, just not on the mat!"

"Brick"
Coach Rick Geist
Foster Brazilian Jiu-Jitsu

1

Filet of Soul

*"Grief is better shared in the light.
Standing in the dark speaks of guilt."*

— Wonder Woman
Comic book #226, author Greg Rucka

"**I**s it good for your soul?" My organic, benevolent, and intellectual friend Susan asked me this question after I spent an afternoon explaining that the bruises on my arms were from my new hobby, Jiu-Jitsu.

I stared at her and shrugged my shoulders. I had not taken the time to think deeply about why I had gravitated toward a sport that appeared rather aggressive. Why did I walk into that padded, red-and-black martial arts gymnasium? It wasn't like I woke up one day, cast my knitting needles aside, and announced, "Today I'm gonna take up combat sports." I had never before participated in a martial art—or any individual sport, for that matter. I didn't watch Ultimate Fighting Championship (UFC) on television. I didn't know what a gi was. I also didn't know that I had walked into that gym to see if I could live fully again.

In April 2007, my universe came crashing down, creating a spiritual vortex that enveloped my sense of caring about myself or my future—my daughter Carly died in my arms from a fatal arrhythmia just a week shy of her fifteenth birthday. In the midst of providing CPR, the arrival of the EMTs, the ambulance ride to the emergency room, and the finality of "I'm so sorry" from the doctors, I lost my faith and my sense of security and entered an empty life, shrouded by the uncertainty of whether or not I mattered anymore.

I began seeing a grief counselor at the insistence of my dearest friends, who also drove me there because I couldn't be alone with my thoughts. Without their persistent compassion, I would have slept all day, drank wine at night, and cried every moment I was awake. I felt as though I was wearing a lead blanket. I did not have the energy or desire to care about anything, least of all myself. Who was there to care about? Who was I, now that Carly was gone?

Carly was my firstborn. She was a precocious child with the ability to focus on tasks for a long period of time. For this reason, she began playing the piano at age four and could read, write, and memorize ahead of her peers. Carly would continue the legacy of her father's family and excel at music, playing not only classical piano, but clarinet and saxophone. She played in the top jazz band and wind ensembles as a freshman in high school. My role in this aspect of her life was simply to listen, watch, encourage, and support. Without even a hint of musical ability myself, I could easily, and equally, be awed by an elementary or high-school performance. Once when I asked Carly about the importance of music in her life, she pointed to a scar on her knee that was shaped like a quarter note and said, "See this, Mom? Music is my destiny."

It was in athletics that Carly was most like me. In fifth grade, Carly approached her father and me and, with her ever-confident tone, told us, "I like soccer, but I really LOVE basketball. So I'm going to just focus on that." And focus she did. In seventh grade, Carly was asked to play on an elite travel team that competed at several national Amateur Athletic Union (AAU) tournaments throughout the year. That first summer, Carly was not a starter on the team. In her mind, she didn't get nearly enough playing time. Instead of pouting like so many kids her age do when things don't go their way, upon her return from the age thirteen and under (U13) Nationals that August, she said, "Take me to the gym. I want to train." And for most of August, Carly spent up to three hours a day with Mo, her coach, improving her shot, ball-handling, footwork, decision making, and passing from the point. She was tenacious, never wanting to stop a drill until she could do the prescribed task correctly. I have always told my children that "hard work pays off." And for Carly it did. That fall during tryouts, people constantly remarked on the improvements to her game. Not only did she start, she led the team in shooting percentage and efficiency (positive stat points per minute of playing time). That spring, after a recruiting tournament in Chicago, Carly received a letter from Notre Dame. It was pretty clear that college basketball was in her future.

It is no secret that I was entrenched in Carly's life. Like Carly at that age, I had made college athletics my goal. Her work ethic reminded me of my own. The only difference was choice of sport: she loved basketball, and I loved volleyball. Her dad and I coached Carly and a team of her school friends from fourth to sixth grade. When Carly began playing on her travel team, she insisted on also playing with her school friends on the original team. This meant four practices a week sometimes, but she never seemed to mind. Staying connected to her friends was a priority for Carly. At one basketball camp they all attended, Carly was asked to "play up" with the high school players, but she turned down the offer, preferring that she and her friends stay together.

I was the "team mom" for the elite team. I traveled to all of the tournaments, attended every practice and training session, and filled in when they needed a "big body" to push around the post players. I loved this life. I was with my daughter, watching her live her dream, and she wanted me there. Before I accepted the assistant's position, I asked her if my close involvement would make her uncomfortable. I didn't want to cramp her style or step on her toes. I wanted her to be free to be herself and did not want to do anything that might taint our relationship. She said, "I want you here. You are my biggest fan." And that is why I was with her the day she died.

We were in North Carolina to play in an NCAA viewing tournament. We had spent the day on the campuses of Duke and the University of

North Carolina. The team had dinner together, and I will never forget that final evening of teenage restaurant antics. All of the laughter, smiling, and lightheartedness were infectious. I will be forever grateful as well for the hug and "thanks for dinner" I got as we left the restaurant.

I remember the first time someone asked me about our final minutes together. I'm sure they were curious to find out if we had been arguing. Earlier that day, Carly had left her cinch bag behind at the Wendy's, where the girls went for lunch. Of course, it was not there when we went back to look for it. In that bag were her new video iPod and my digital camera that was a birthday present from my parents, which she had borrowed without my permission. Everyone knew that her oversight weighed heavily on her mind. One of my favorite pictures of Carly was taken in the Duke cathedral. She is in the second pew, holding hands with her two best friends, eyes squeezed shut as she prays to find her bag.

That evening, back in the hotel room, she was lounging on her bed, hair wet from the shower, Reese's Peanut Butter Cup wrapper in her lap, talking to her boyfriend on her cell phone. I overhead her lamenting to Tyler about her situation, and I walked to the end of the bed to get her attention and said, "Carly, let it go. YOU are so much more important than THINGS." It was maybe five minutes later after she hung up that a strange noise made me look over my shoulder. She was having an irreversible arrhythmia.

A lot of what you hear about death and grieving sounds cliché until it is happening to you. There is a saying, "Let not the sun go down upon your anger." I believe it was by the grace of God that my last words to Carly were words of love and comfort. I hope she took them with her and, in her new role as guardian angel, can whisper wisdom into the ears of people who are in the midst of death, so that they will not suffer the torment of unkind last words.

"My heart
Where did you go?
Wounded companion went
Away from me to bathe in tears
Come back."

— Elena Stowell

2

Family Mug Shot

"I know. It's going to be OK. We're going to get better. We're going to heal. And everything's going to be OK."

— Wonder Woman
Comic book #175, Phil Jiminez

Most people think that Chuck and I are complete opposites. We probably are. I met Chuck while I was a student teacher of biology at a high school in Kent, Washington. Chuck was the band director. This was also the high school that Chuck had attended as a teenager and the same high school in which his father had been the band director.

There is a lot of musical genius on Chuck's side. I am musical only if I don't sing or try to play an instrument. When the kids were little, Chuck told me I had a lovely voice (tolerable), but to please not sing in front of the children. I did not think it was possible to sing "Old McDonald" out of tune, but apparently it is. In an effort to preserve prodigal possibilities, I complied.

Family gatherings on the Stowell side are intimidating. When the invitation says "Charlie D, bring your trumpet," I know that I will join the other "married ins" as a wallflower. I recall the lineup one Christmas: Tom on piano; Rosie, oboe; Marlys, flute and vocals; Danielle, French horn (full ride to Julliard); Evan, bassoon (full ride to Julliard); and Danielle's boyfriend at the time, trombone (professional symphony player). Marlys rifled through a pile of music—"How 'bout this?"—and gave everyone a sheet. Chuck said, "Hey, this is clarinet music." And they started in on Handel's Messiah. Chuck transposed it all to trumpet on the fly. (Transposing while playing is the equivalent of turning a book written in a foreign language upside down and reading it as fast as everyone else who is reading a copy in English.) I don't rate even a triangle, but I do know when to clap.

The paths of a potential science teacher and a music guy were not destined to cross within the confines of the main building on campus. I didn't know where the band room was, and Chuck passed the science wing on his way to the staff mailboxes. We met coaching basketball. I had volunteered with the volleyball team, and so when the girls' basketball program was short a coach, I was asked to help out. Chuck was tall and quiet when not coaching. When he did talk, he was really funny. I found this intriguing. He drove a sports car, and the girls on the team accused me of being a "tire-biter" when we became an item, but we had gotten to know each other the way many sports people do: over beers after the games.

We didn't share many beers after we got married because I got pregnant right away. Remember how I said Chuck was funny? One of my OB/GYN appointments was on April 1, and my OB/GYN was an old basketball buddy of Chuck's. Unbeknownst to me, Chuck had arrived early to my appointment, got the ultrasound nurse to point out multiple sets of arms and legs (all looked fuzzy to me), and had me convinced I was having twins. I cried, "How are we going to do this?" . . . "No wonder I'm so huge" . . . "I'll never work again." Chuck patted my hand, saying, "Isn't this great?" The nurse who was in on the joke was smiling, and then the doctor popped in. They all yelled, "April Fools." If I had known Jiu-Jitsu at that time, I would have choked him out.

Chuck doesn't make many requests, but when we first found out I was pregnant, he told me that if we had a daughter, he had always wanted to name her Carly Dawn because his family calls him Charlie Don. Eighteen days after that hilarious April afternoon, Carly Dawn was born on Easter morning. We always told her that she arrived in my Easter basket.

Our family rounded out with the births of Eason (named after me, E's son) and Carson (a hybrid of Carly and Eason). The kids were all involved in sports and music and followed a typical birth-order pattern. Carly was driven and wanted to try everything. With robust passion, she would bound down the stairs and ask, "What's the schedule?" Eason liked to blend in and not draw any attention to himself, except that he had a pestering way of contradicting everyone just to get a rise out of us. We used to call him Carl Contrary. Carson was a model youngest child. He flourished in that sense of security that youngest children often have. He learned from the errors of his older siblings what to say, or not to say, to make mom happy and get what he wanted. Chuck and I were blessed to have a brood that was sincerely each other's best friend.

Mothers and daughters share a special bond—special, but not always easy. Carly and I butted heads for a while, like in most such relationships—particularly with two headstrong women in the same household. We played a lot of family basketball in the backyard, and when Carly realized she could dribble and shoot much better than I, things between us smoothed out. I think that was about sixth grade. After that, her transgressions ranged from tipping back on her chair at the dinner table, texting her friends after bedtime, and constantly forgetting to put enough to drink in her gym bag.

Chuck and Carly spoke the language of music, and I was left completely out of that. They would disappear for hours, writing music and practicing. I never ceased to be amazed by how they could listen to something and then start playing it within minutes, adding their own personal touches. Truly a gift.

Boys are different, but the bond is nonetheless special. From my boys, I learned that Lego is not a toy, it's a lifestyle; that there is a meat-to-bun sandwich ratio that must never be deviated from; and that "yo Mom-Dawg" is a term of endearment.

Carly's passion for life and for having fun sticks with us to this day. She loved practical jokes, like her father. She would stick her head out the window and bark like a dog—just because it was fun. Her friends still do this on her birthday to honor her.

3

Fresh off the Couch

The first three months of my grief, I wanted to disappear. I didn't want to die, but I didn't care if I lived. I had paralyzing social anxiety. I felt like everyone could see through me to my bare and irreparable broken heart. I did not return to work. This was my first example that people grieve differently. My husband went back to work right away. He found comfort in keeping his routine the same. As Carly's band teacher, his classroom was full of Carly's music friends who had known her since kindergarten. He wanted them to know that he was okay and that they would be okay. I found that admirable.

I, on the other hand, could have cared less if anyone else was okay because I was at the lowest point of my existence. By this time, I had become puffy with twenty extra pounds of depression around my midsection. I had gone through a couple of cases of wine and several books about "the afterlife," which people apparently felt compelled to give me. I couldn't keep two thoughts straight in my head. My body was in the house, but I wasn't there.

If asked, most people would remember me on the couch. But I had crazy manic episodes too. I would become the whirling dervish of Kent, Washington, moving constantly at a frenetic pace. I couldn't sit still. I would sit, get up, putter around, write for hours, sit—heart racing, my insides shaking. If someone else was around, I would talk and talk and talk about anything. This was just an active way of distracting myself from what I didn't want to think about. I could sleep the day away or fill it with superficial activities so that I never stopped moving. I didn't set out to act this way—"Hmm, today feels like a manic Monday"—but I would get caught up in it before I knew it.

One time, when I couldn't sleep, I was pacing around downstairs when I got this wild hair to go to our exercise room and see if I could bench 115 pounds. I have no idea where that number came from (my maximum was only 105 pounds), but I was determined. I scrambled around, trying to find the plates I needed to get 115 pounds on the bar. Plates were clanking, and just as I was ready to grab the bar, Chuck walked in. "What are you doing? It's two a.m." I looked at him as if I do this every day and said, "How 'bout a spot?" Chuck just shook his head, admonished, "Don't hurt yourself," and walked away. Chuck doesn't lift weights.

During a session with Kathleen, my grief therapist, she remarked that I seemed like a person who needed to move and who functioned best when I was connected to my body. How did she know this? From my chronic fidgeting, leg-crossing, finger-tapping, and exhaustive crying? Did she see me lift weights in the middle of the night? Was this why she often forced me to take a walk before I got into my car to drive home? When I told her that I was thinking of calling a number I saw for women to join a boot camp fitness group in my area, she looked at me as if I told her I saw the Virgin Mary in a tortilla.

To an outsider, most of our sessions up to this point would have played out like reruns: I cry. She says, "Breathe." I cry and say, "I can't do it anymore." She says, "Yes you can." I cry, "When will I feel better?" She says, "When you are ready." I cry, "Am I crazy?" She says, "No, there is no right or wrong way to grieve, only your way. There is no manual for you to follow." I cry, "This is hard." She says, "I know."

When she had regained her *therapistic* composure (yes, I made that word up) after my comment about boot camp, she said, "Let me know how it goes." I replied. "I probably won't do it." And right then, I knew that I would. I used reverse psychology on myself.

*"If you start pretending to have fun,
you might even have a little by accident."*

— Alfred Pennyworth to Bruce Wayne
From the movie *Batman Begins* 2005

My parents were elated to hear that I was considering an activity other than sleeping. At the time, I didn't realize how difficult all this was for them. Not only had they lost their first grandchild, but they were losing their daughter as well. My dad sent me a check paying for six months of the camp (I had told him I was going to try it for a month) as a birthday present. Everybody is a shrink.

I loathe exercising in the morning, and boot camp was at five-thirty in the morning. Add depression and my-fat-self to someone who does not pop out of bed like toast, and you have a recipe for grumpy. I showed up on time, but I didn't talk much and preferred to just do my reps without being bothered. I didn't need to talk. I didn't need any new friends. I was there to work out. I would work out until six-thirty, and then go home and go back to bed. In my mind, I could check off "move today" from my list of appeasements to others.

Despite how unfriendly I appeared, I was asked to join a team traveling to British Columbia to compete in FemSport. It's a competition where you compete in different exercises against one other person, and your scores are compiled for an individual score and a team score. The events were bicep curls in one minute at 30% body weight; fifty 18" box jumps for time; weighted sled pull at 65% body weight; kettle bell shuttle where the bells got progressively heavier and the pedestals you put them on got higher; and an obstacle course where you carried jugs of water, flipped tires, walked a balance beam, and sprinted.

I was the heaviest competitor in the event at 203 pounds. I was appalled at weigh-in. I had never weighed that much without being pregnant. At FemSport, that meant I was going to have to lift and curl and drag more weight than anyone in the competition. To my credit,

I beat my opponent in all the events and finished in the middle of the pack in points. I guess there were still some muscles under all that insulation. But all I could think about was being the heaviest person in the meet.

The director had said, "Well, someone has to be the heaviest." Easy to say when the heaviest thing about you is your clipboard. I went out and had Jagermeister shots that night.

4

My Rubber Room

Some tangled occurrences led me to the Foster Brazilian Jiu-Jitsu gym. At times during boot camp, we would change it up by doing some cardio kickboxing. I thought it was really fun, although no one wanted to be my partner because afterward their hands hurt from holding the mitts. Even the most athletic gals in the group were much smaller than me, so I had to "pull my punches," so to speak.

Around this time, Kathleen suggested that I was not admitting to feelings of anger and that it was unhealthy to hold them in. I could deal with this, she instructed, by first finding a place where I could not hurt myself—what, a rubber room?—and then punch a pillow, or perhaps go into the forest and scream. Although I was nodding to make her happy, inside I was rolling my eyes and thinking, LAME. Those tactics were clearly not going to be part of my wellness plan.

I had decided, thanks to the boot camp introduction to kickboxing, that I wanted to learn how to kick and punch correctly (not like a girlie-girl) and do it someplace where I wouldn't have to hold back. As serendipity would have it, during some downtime while teaching my high-school biology class, I googled "kickboxing Kent WA." The website for Foster Brazilian Jiu-Jitsu was on my screen when one of my students walked behind me and said, "Hey Foster's. I go there. My dad is one of the coaches." My student, the daughter of one of the coaches there and a charismatic, athletic young lady, went on to tell me where the gym was located and convinced me that everyone there was treated like family.

Who wudda thunk it? At the very moment Foster BJJ was on my screen, someone who had trained there would see me looking at it. Coincidence? I think not.

> *"Life's challenges are not supposed to paralyze you, they're supposed to help you discover who you are."*
>
> — Bernice Johnson Reagan

The first lesson was free, so I emailed the coach, James Foster, and signed up to try the striking class. Striking is taught by Bobi D., a Swedish former boxer and Jiu-Jitsu brown belt. Coach calls him Blue Steel due to his inability to take a bad photograph.

I soaked it all up—the repetitive footwork drills, the ducking-under drills that made my quads burn, punching combinations into the mitts, cardio punching the heavy bag until I couldn't lift my arms. I loved it. I didn't know what heavy-handed meant, but I was called that. Intent on practicing, I bought a heavy bag so that I could get more reps in and chalked lines in the garage to practice my footwork. I downloaded boxing workouts, and I would go out into our cold basement to jump rope and do intervals of punch combinations. It was a winter distraction for me. Winter is tough because that's basketball season.

> *"In three words I can sum up everything I've learned about life: It goes on."*
>
> — Robert Frost

I didn't watch girls' basketball for three years after Carly died because I physically couldn't. The first time I tried to watch her AAU team play, I had to take two laps outside the gym before I could enter.

I was composed until I saw all of the players from her club wearing patches displaying "21," Carly's number. I had to leave and go throw up. I tried again during high-school basketball season. Like AAU, the parents and teammates all insisted they wanted to see me there. I would smile and greet people, and then I'd let my eyes stray to the large shadowbox on the gymnasium wall, where her retired jersey hangs with a plaque that says, "An artist on and off the court," and my throat would seal up and my chest would implode and I would feel like I couldn't breathe.

I continued to have these panic attacks for years around girls' basketball, a sport I loved and missed, but could never feel the same way about again. Eventually I distracted myself with coaching volleyball and scheduling practices on Fridays so I had an excuse for not being able to accept the invitations to the games. My boys both play basketball and wear #21 in their sister's honor. Watching Carson play ball does déjà-vu with my heart. He looks just like Carly with his long, gangly body and fluid gestures. They share many of the same court mannerisms, like pacing behind the free-throw line while waiting, and rocking back and forth on their toes in the huddle—wound tight like a racehorse pawing at the starting gate. Going to see the boys play is not as hard as watching the girls, but still I don't watch many of their games. I prefer to stay at home and get their texts, "Mom, I scored twenty-one points! I know Carly was there with me." People say they understand. I'm not sure I understand. Sometimes I ask myself why I am not over it yet. I feel guilty about not being there. Yes, I feel like a bad mom.

Bad mom, but better boxer—or so I thought. One time at practice, I had been there maybe six weeks when one of the other coaches, Rick, suggested that I spar with Bobi. Here begins the lesson in controlling one's enthusiasm and spastic behavior. Heavy bags and mitts are one thing, but they don't punch you back.

Apparently I got a bit too vigorous (Bobi was jabbing me over and over again. It was maddening!), and Bobi popped me on the side of the head, pretty hard. Then he stopped the class. "Hey, just so you know, when you are training, your partner will go as hard as you go. So if you dish it out, then you better be able to take it." *Uhhh, that's directed at me, isn't it?* I would later realize that stopping a class to point something out for the benefit of the whole class was Foster standard operating procedure. One has to understand that it's not personal, even though you know you started it.

5

Lucky Charms of Remembrance

L oss can be especially painful for people who have emotional attachments to inanimate objects. I was that child who cried when her brothers tied her favorite stuffed animal in a ball and kicked it around the house. "Stop it. You are hurting Huggy Bubbles." I had such an attachment and love for this more-than-an-object stuffed animal that "Huggy" became Carly's nickname within the family. And yes, I still have Huggy Bubbles, although Chuck refuses to let me bring her into the bed.

I'm not attached to just any old thing. I'm not ready to be featured on *Buried Alive* (the show about hoarders), but I am very sentimental about gifts I have been given or objects that remind me of someone or a special time. I can still look at an old wedding present and tell you who gave it to us twenty years later. I can find meaning in the simplest of trinkets if one of my children gave it to me. I can tell you where I was when I picked up a piece of art or handmade jewelry. And so deciding what to do with Carly's things was like a storm cloud that followed me around the house, threatening to cause turmoil at whatever I perceived to be the slightest disturbance to my coping.

The first time I saw the door to Carly's room ajar, I was angry. Who went in there? Why did you go in? It turned out that the boys had gone in to pay tribute to Carly by raiding her extensive collection of Jordan basketball shorts. I became aware of this one morning when Eason came into the kitchen wearing the green and gray shorts that matched Carly's favorite pair of J's—her Green Beans. I remember catching my breath with a silent gasp. I wanted to react sharply. I was shocked, angry, betrayed, caught off guard. Yet, I just sat there. Somewhere amidst those edgy feelings, I realized that this was perfectly acceptable, a discreet way for a young teenage boy to pay homage to his sister. Who was I to stop him from doing that? It was too painful for him to talk about, but he wanted everyone to know that he missed her and carried her with him.

I went crazy trying to carry her with me by wearing symbolic talismans—rituals I was sure would tell her that I hadn't left her, that I would remember her and miss her every moment.

I wore a silver necklace with a butterfly, a cross, and the number 21 in a heart every day . . . for a long time.

I still wear a leather bracelet with the words Gratitude, Forgiveness, Courage, Acceptance, and Kindness on it. I look at it most days as a measure of my emotional status. Gratitude, for the time I had with her: okay today. Forgiveness: nope, not there yet. Courage: going forward today? Yes. Acceptance: sometimes. Kindness to others, like she often gave: I can do this. How I answer varies from day to day.

I found an artist who made dichroic glass pendants and had her make some in shades of blue and emerald that contained bits of Carly's ashes and gave one each to my brothers and my parents and put two away for the boys. I had mine mounted in silver and engraved with her name and "Ah be boo" on the back. Like most little kids, Carly had her own language for a while, and "Ah be boo" was her way of saying "I love you." At night, we played the Waltons, yelling it through the walls to one another. I wore this pendant or carried it with me every day that first year of survival. I felt that I was never far away from her.

And then I got a tattoo. Like the powerful need I had to wear or carry symbols of her with me, I felt I had to immortalize her. On my lower leg, I have her motto: "Do what you love, love what you do" with a basketball and a 21, a blue butterfly, and a music note. It seems that tattooing a memory is not uncommon, and Carly's friends and coaches have paid tribute to her with their own tattoos. There are butterflies, 21s, a twenty-one in script, and a basketball with Carly's name. One friend had "Do what you love, love what you do" tattooed across her ribs. I feel so honored and humbled by these acts; they let me know that I am not alone in missing her and that Carly made a difference to many people. Not to be left out, Chuck had his dentist put a 21 on his new crown.

Over time, I began to accept that neither my world nor my composure would fall apart if I didn't wear one of my talismans. I stopped feeling guilty if I left them in my jewelry box. But I still have problems with family pictures. I don't have a problem with pictures of the boys, or the boys with Chuck, or Chuck and me, or the boys and me, but I dislike pictures of the four of us together, because they just don't look right. The pictures seem like an incomplete family, and I only see who is missing. I don't have a single picture of our "new" family displayed either. I don't know, I just can't . . . yet.

And what of Carly's things? Most are still in the same place. I have been able to give away some of her clothes by walking into her room and telling myself, "Oh, this wouldn't fit any more," but I leave everything else: the pictures of her friends, her trophies, favorite books, journals, Beanie Babies, and basketball shoes. I still burst into tears when I unexpectedly find a spiral notebook with her writing in it, a doodle on a pad of paper, an old card she'd given me.

I've had people ask me what I've done with Carly's room. That frustrates and irritates me. Kathleen has told me that I can take all the time I need . . . and that when it's time, I will know. It is not discussed in our house. I know, without it ever being spoken, that it is up to me to decide.

Having attachments to symbols has served me well in Jiu-Jitsu. The martial arts are full of symbolic rituals and emblems, and somehow, this comforts me. Before comfort, however, came baptism by fire, so to speak. Never having been a martial arts practitioner, I did not know many of these rituals and learned of them after many an innocent, yet reprimandable gaffe. For instance, I thought that if I was late, I should hurry, put on my uniform, and jump into the warmup. No! If you are late, you must stand patiently on the edge of the mat until the instructor notices you and gives you permission to join in. When you have permission, you must bow, step on the mat, and depending on how late you are, either join the line or have a private workout session on the side, which is called "ropes." Nobody likes to do ropes. First off, it's just you, singled out because of your tardiness, and the upper belt, who gets the privilege of holding the rope. The rope is tied to a section of cage and held about eighteen inches off the ground. You must jump over and back sideways, over and back frontward and backward, and then you must drop to your belly, crawl under the rope without touching it, and jump up and over the rope again. The magic number of repetitions depends on how late you were and whether or not Coach has had a nice day. I've done at least twenty a couple of times.

There is symbolism and honor attached to your uniform. Your uniform, called a gi, must be clean, neat, and properly adjusted any time you are lined up to bow. The belt is the most important and symbolic part of the uniform. Your belt tells everyone your rank. Your rank signifies your level of achievement in the sport. One of the rituals I learned was that you are to never wash your belt. A belt that looks "used" indicates that the wearer has trained hard for a long time. Each gym also has team patches. Getting a team patch was very important to me. As in any sport, wearing the insignia of your gym means that you "represent." I was especially proud to receive my Competition Team patch. It's amazing how a piece of fabric can make you feel like you belong.

Getting back to tattoos: A great number of Jiu-Jitsu folks have tattoos. Most have more than one. And I'm sure if I asked them, each person could tell me the meaning behind each piece of body art. I can feel that. Interestingly, Coach is not in favor of people getting tattoos of the gym logo or Lotus Club, our parent organization. He says members will typically ask him if they should; he suggests they do not; they go ahead anyway; and then they either quit or move away and join another gym. Well, I would get a tattoo of our gym. I would because I am fiercely loyal and owe my life to this gym. I'm pretty sure that if I moved away from here I wouldn't roll anymore. I know I ended up at Foster because I was supposed to, because I needed to. Maybe if I win a gold medal, I'll get one. Should I ask Coach for permission or forgiveness?

6

Off the Couch and
on the Mat

I had been striking for a few weeks when Coach Rick asked me
to come and watch a Jiu-Jitsu class. "What's that?" I had never
even heard of Jiu-Jitsu except that it was in the gym name. And
I had never seen a class because striking class was the last class of
the day. I was enjoying striking just fine and didn't see a need to add
anything else to my repertoire. But he was persistent. He wore me
down.

About Rick: Rick is big. Let's say, maybe six-two, 270 on a slim day.
Hence his nickname Brick—Big Rick. When Brick is not rolling, he
is a welding instructor. I think it's a combination of genetics and the
constant use of heavy equipment that gives Brick forearms the size of
most mortals' calves. When Brick puts on a baseball choke, you have
to tap or its "broken bat" lights out. (It takes 5,000 pounds of impact
force to break a bat, and only 38 pounds to break a neck . . . science
geekism.)

Brick has his own tale of moxie. In January 2009 (the day before
his forty-ninth birthday), the inconvenience of a nagging headache
sent Brick to the doctors. Instead of the prescription pain reliever he
expected, Brick wound up in neurosurgery to have a brain tumor the
size of a tangerine removed. The tumor didn't kill him, but not being
able to roll almost did. He had to wait six months for his skull bones
to heal before he got the green light to hit the mats again. I might also
add that it took about six months for him to grow enough hair to end
his Frankenstein impersonation.

Brick also complained about "losing too much weight," because he couldn't work out. Is that another insult to feminism or what? I had to work my ass off to literally work my ass off. Apparently, if I was Brick, I could have put a dent in the couch and bought a smaller pair of jeans.

The pinnacle of his recovery is that a year or so later Brick competed in the Pan Jiu-Jitsu Championships and won two gold medals, one in his weight division Senior 3 age 44 and up, and one in the Open, where all weights compete together in that age bracket. Coach also promoted him to brown belt.

So one day, I went to watch a no-gi Jiu-Jitsu class, which is also called submission grappling. A few thoughts came to mind: Whoa, that's a lot of touching; those guys are really sweaty—slimy-looking actually; looks kinda aggressive. I played collegiate volleyball, which is a non-contact sport. Basketball and touch football were the only level of contact sports I was familiar with, and they were "normal," because at least they involved a ball.

Brick: "When we gonna see you again? What are you doing Saturday morning? Come and watch another class." At that point in my life, there wasn't much filling my weekends, and Brick smiles like he really does want to see you again, so I went to watch.

"You must do the thing you think you cannot do."
— Eleanor Roosevelt

This was a gi class, so everyone was wearing their martial arts uniform that resembles a judo uniform. A gi is built for functionality. It is made of sturdy cotton in a weave that can take plenty of abuse. The jacket folds over in the front like a kimono and has a sturdy lapel. The lapel is a favorite place on the gi to "get your grips," and it is thicker than the rest of the jacket. The pants have a drawstring and gusseted crotch so that you have plenty of freedom to move—and probably so that you don't split your pants when you are in compromising positions that put a strain on the seams. The third piece is the belt. There is a special way to tie your belt, and it is very important that you tie it correctly. I looked it up on YouTube to make sure I had it right. To not tie your belt correctly or to drag it on the ground is dishonorable.

Brick noticed I was wearing sweats, so he invited me to join the warmup. Okay, I can run in a circle, no big deal. But then they started getting down on the mat and doing line drills and contorting their bodies in ways unfamiliar to me. Sensing the questioning look on my face, I was taken aside and taught some basic moves and vocabulary.

That day, I learned how to "shrimp" and hold someone in "side control." ("Mount" was seriously suspect.) I still wasn't sold. I certainly was not going to wear one of those uniforms. It looked very cumbersome and hot. But I was nagged by the voice that anyone who has competed knows; the one that says, "You can do that. If you don't even try it, then you have failed." I bought a pair of fight shorts (which I thought were pretty cool) and started going to the no-gi class that was scheduled before the striking class.

It turned out that submission grappling was as slimy as it looked. And there was touching for pretty much the entire one and a half hours. And there were no other girls usually. Being the only woman most of the time didn't bother me. I grew up in the middle between two brothers. I was also the only girl on the block growing up, so I played with the boys. I grew fast and was taller than most of the boys as well. I remember always being in the middle of the back row for pictures in elementary school. I went on to play three varsity sports all four years of high school and played year-round club volleyball. Needless to say, I was no stranger to a gym or to being challenged by boys to athletic competitions. I could trash-talk and "good old boy" with the best of them. In graduate school, I was the only woman to join the faculty and other graduate students for "a run"—gym-speak for playing lunchtime basketball. This continued throughout my adult life. I played on two three-on-three teams (one was coed) at Hoopfest in Spokane two months after giving birth to Carly. And yes, I breast-fed between games. (Ah, but I digress to my younger days.)

Eventually I bought a gi. A blue one because most of the people wore white and that seemed rather bland. In my mind, this uniform meant commitment. I told myself that I would give Brazilian Jiu-Jitsu (BJJ) a year. A year would be enough time to gauge my aptitude and feel like I gave it an honest try. And so my journey began.

7

It Really is a Journey

L et me stop for a minute and talk about "the journey." We all know the saying, "it's about the journey, not the destination." In the gym during promotions, Coach would often remind everyone that we each had a personal Jiu-Jitsu journey, and it was not about rank or promotions. Some people advance quickly; some people take awhile. We all have differing backgrounds in martial arts, athleticism, and fitness, and we all have varying learning curves. People also have different schedules. Some people can train every day and others only once a week. For these reasons, the coach emphasized the importance of not comparing yourself to others or focusing on the next belt. He would remind us to come to class when we could, train hard, and do our best, and the rest would fall into place when the time was right.

Yes, I believed this wholeheartedly, but not deeply. Each day I was able to train, I was simply thankful to have made it through another class—because my measure at the time was just to participate in the world again, to be consistent about something. I wasn't thinking about rank or promotions because I only thought about life one day at a time—just moving forward for twenty-four hours. That was my status quo for a year and a half. If I thought too far ahead, I would fall apart.

The anticipation of significant dates or holidays would trigger terrible anxiety. Carly's birthday and the day she died are only one week apart in April. My anxiety would start to creep in around the middle of March. By the first week of April, I would have trouble sleeping, start eating poorly, and start drinking more, and I would become "the weeping woman." A song by the Fray (Carly's favorite band) would play, and I would cry. People sent cards and emails and texts, and each one was bittersweet. I was glad they remembered her and me, but each one was like a little dagger into my heart, just tormenting me with how much I missed her. For most of April, I felt like crap. I wouldn't train much because physically I felt ghastly, and emotionally I wasn't sure I could keep it together for an hour and a half. If I let my mind wander to my grief, I would start crying. And there's no crying on the mat. That I might not be able to keep it together just made me more anxious.

> *The harder the conflict, the more glorious the triumph.*
>
> — Thomas Paine

It was probably close to my second year of Jiu-Jitsu, three years after Carly's death, that I began to realize that I could shrug off some of the weight of the world that kept me yoked. I can recall a speech of sorts I gave at a fundraiser for The Carly Stowell Foundation. It went something like this:

People who have known me for a while know that I am prone to curious etiquette. I have a Happy Birthday banner that hangs across a beam in our living room—everyday—for years. A few times I started to take it down, and then I'd begin to feel a little blue. I'd think, "It's somebody's birthday today, and won't they be sad if they don't have a banner?" And so the banner stayed there. I would also send thank you cards to my friends at Thanksgiving, usually enclosing a small rock or trinket that made me think of them. I would write a memory I shared with them inside the card and tell them how thankful I was to have them in my life. Well, I stopped doing that after Carly died. I quite simply did not feel thankful for any part of my life anymore. It felt like my grief was a heavy stone, and I was being crushed underneath it. It was hard to breathe or move under the weight of it. Yet it protected me.

After a while, I was able to crawl out from under the stone. I could breathe more easily. Still, I felt like I had picked up the stone and put it in a backpack that I carried everywhere. Grief "had my back," but not in a good way. I could move, but grief still weighed me down.

And now, I finally feel like I can take that stone out of my backpack and leave it for a while. I can rejoin the world, lighter and for longer than before. And for this, I am thankful. Thank you for helping me move the stone. Thank you for carrying the backpack when I could not. I'll be writing those thank you cards once again.

> *"Great love and great achievement involve great risk."*
>
> — A Dalai Lama wisdom

I had made it through two Aprils with a gi on. And each one was a little easier. I still "fell off the rails," but each time I fell a little less far. Other people started to point out to me the mileage I was adding to my journey. I remember last fall, one of my colleagues tentatively said, "Stowell, you seem different." I replied, "Yeah, I feel like I can think clearly for the first time in a long time." My doctor (who did not know me pre-grief) said, "You have a joie de vivre I have never seen in you." I felt healthier, stronger, and more confident, and I said, "It's the Jiu-Jitsu."

8
Brazilian Jiu-Jitsu 101

When you think of "martial arts," what comes to mind? Jackie Chan and Bruce Lee fending off entire gangs of miscreants? Samurai with their topknot hairdos and mighty swords? A park lawn dotted with senior citizens peacefully executing the katas of tai chi? A guy in a white uniform breaking boards with his bare hand? Or perhaps turtles cloaked in black, hurling throwing stars and swinging nunchuks?

Many cultures have a martial arts tradition. The oldest martial arts are believed to have originated as long ago as 3,000 BC in Korea and China. Many styles that are practiced today have not changed significantly since their inception. Each style differs in its external movements, but all of the martial arts embrace the axiom of a spiritual endeavor.

Brazilian Jiu-Jitsu (BJJ), being rather young, has a distinct and traceable path. It is believed by some that Japanese old-style Jujutsu, an unarmed form of combat used by samurai, is the parent martial art of BJJ. In 1915, Japanese immigrant Esai Maeda taught the skills of Japanese Jujutsu to Carlos Gracie in Brazil. Carlos continued to teach the Japanese art and established the first Gracie Jiu-Jitsu academy in Rio de Janeiro in 1925. Helio, Carlos's younger brother, was fascinated by the sport, but was restricted from practicing the techniques due to his small size and fragile frame.

Determined to participate, Helio refined and adapted the Japanese-style art he spent years observing. His goals were to make Jiu-Jitsu more suitable to his lack of strength and smaller size by developing techniques that employed leverage, timing, and coordinated body movements. In 1928, together with his brother Carlos, they took an existing martial art and advanced it into what we now refer to as BJJ.

BJJ can be practiced by just about anyone; Helio Gracie is the original example of this. You will see a variety of body types in a BJJ class: tall, petite, robust, lean, sturdy, buffed, and scrawny. You will see participants of all ages: kids as young as four years old, teens, adults, and masters. Helio Gracie was still competing in his fifties.

Most of BJJ happens after a match or altercation is taken to the ground. This is what makes BJJ distinguishable from other martial arts. The main focus is often referred to as the "ground game." The techniques of BJJ focus on the principles of leverage, balance, and timing, allowing those of smaller stature or limited athletic ability to defend themselves against larger and stronger opponents. The art of BJJ is comprised of many sweeps, reversals, chokes, arm locks, and leg locks.

A typical training session at a BJJ gym has three phases and begins with the students lining up by rank to face and bow to the instructor, who is often a black belt in the art. First, the students are led through a warmup beginning with jogging and some general conditioning exercises, such as push-ups, squats, burpees, and core work. Next, the students practice movements that are foundational to many BJJ techniques: shrimping, technical stand-ups, shoulder rolls, and bridging. By this point, the average person's heart rate will have risen and the sweating would have started, just in time to start learning a new technique.

During the second phase, a new technique, or two, is taught to the students. A skillful instructor will demonstrate the technique step by step and explain just enough nuances for the students to be successful but not overwhelmed. Students then partner up and drill. For people new to the sport, this can be the awkward part. It is during drill that you must get up-close-and-personal with another student. If you have a strong resistance to people entering your personal bubble, this sport will not be for you. Depending upon the technique, you may have someone sitting on top of you, have their legs wrapped around your waist, or have their face very close to your crotch or other oft-considered private place. BJJ is an excellent catalyst for personal hygiene.

Drilling in BJJ is critical to success. The initial stages of learning the art can be very frustrating. BJJ is complex. Anyone with longevity in the sport has most certainly had their patience tested several times. There are myriad techniques and details to master, and people who expect to be good right away typically do not last. A student who finds excitement in the creativity and challenge of each technique will return time and time again. Instructors of the art relish the veritable opportunity within BJJ to develop new transitions, technique variations, countermeasures, and submissions. BJJ is a dynamic sport that continues to grow and change.

A training session usually ends with sparring. Sparring allows the student to practice the techniques with near-100% resistance without "pulling any punches," so to speak. If a student is caught in a choke, armlock, or leg lock, they simply tap out and continue training injury free. This allows the student to practice the techniques in a life-like situation so they can be confident that they would recall a technique in a real self-defense or competitive situation.

Although the main focus of BJJ is self-defense, the style has also grown into an extremely popular sport. BJJ competitions are held across the world with the major events registering thousands of competitors. The competitions are often referred to as "Sport BJJ" tournaments and should not be confused with mixed martial arts (MMA) events.

Sport BJJ matches start similar to a wrestling or Judo match, with both competitors standing and working for the takedown or other technique to get the match to the ground. As with many other sports, there is a set of rules in place to keep the athletes safe. There is also a point system, though the ultimate victory is to force your opponent to submit, often referred to as "tapping out," using a variety of submission holds. Athletes compete based upon the criteria of weight, rank, age, and gender. Because there are far fewer woman who compete, we most often do not have the luxury of age divisions.

BJJ is also an integral part of a modern-day MMA competitor's skill set. BJJ for MMA differs slightly from Sport BJJ because of additional strikes and the lack of a uniform. However, the fundamental escapes, submissions, counters, and reversals comprise a large part of most of the top MMA athlete's ground game today. It's important to note that the modern-day MMA athlete needs to be well versed in all areas, and there is no single style that is the best for all situations.

9

White Belt Blues

[Luke] "What's in there?"
[Yoda] "Only what you take with you."

— Star Wars Episode V:
The Empire Strikes Back (1980)

"The theme of the white belt is survival, nothing more, nothing less," says Saulo Ribeiro in *Jiu-Jitsu University*. This author describes a white belt as an empty vessel with no one against which to compare oneself. Everyone begins Jiu-Jitsu as a white belt. My belt felt *really* white. Before a white belt can move on, they must become a survivor. Ribeiro describes the white-belt level as the time when a student's insecurity and patience will be tested. White belts do not have a lot of skill yet, but if they are smart and focus on their defense and knowledge, they can survive. Ribeiro's words are a poignant complement to the last four years of my life, as I struggled to survive the anguish of my daughter's sudden death.

When I started rolling, I was damaged goods. I had a broken heart, low confidence, and high anxiety; I didn't believe I was worth my time. After a couple of weeks of Jiu-Jitsu, I was even more damaged—physically. I popped a rib cartilage learning to "escape from mount," and it hurt to cough, laugh, and ... well, breathe. But I had committed in my mind to a year, so I wrapped my ribs in a six-inch-wide bandage and told myself that when I healed, I seriously needed to work on my core. I still wanted to go in—even with the injury—because the gym had become part of my routine. My parents called it therapeutic (this made me smirk at the time). I looked forward to my Thursday night to myself, when I could work up a good cleansing sweat. My dear friend Kelly liked to tell everyone I was a cage fighter. She also thought it was funny to ask me, loudly, in public places, "How is your BJ (long pause) J class going?" Very funny. I had to keep telling everyone I was not a cage fighter and my husband that I only rolled with women (heh heh). No one really cared why I was going. Already they were seeing a difference in me that I could not yet see in myself. Apparently I was in recovery, but I was the last to know.

One of my other early BJJ injuries was to my shoulder. A big Samoan guy put me in a keylock/Americana (see Jiu-Jitsu University, page 330) with a bit too much enthusiasm. My shoulder was painful to use for a couple of weeks. But things were going okay, and I was able to participate mostly using my other arm—that is, until we sparred. I was set to spar with a strong and experienced guy. I asked him to watch my shoulder, and I was having difficulty doing moves. He made the remark, "You shouldn't be here."

I was devastated and bolted out of the gym as soon as class ended, trying not to cry. Of course my wounded state of mind was telling me that he was right. *What was I doing there? I couldn't do it. I'm hurt and I'm not any good and I'm a wussy because I'm crying.* I should have been captain of the negative self-talk team. By this time in my grief journey, I was an expert at driving while crying, so I started to leave the parking lot when I heard the beep that indicated I had a text. It was Coach asking me if I was okay. "No!" I replied, and I texted him my tale of woe and how unfriendly "that guy" was.

Of course, it turned out that the guy merely meant that I should stay home and take care of my arm until it is healed. But I was at this overly sensitive time in my life, and beating up on myself was the only fight I knew I could win.

10

Coach and His Guns

"A leader is one who knows the way,
goes the way, and shows the way."

— John C. Maxwell

Coach James Foster, "Coach," is an imposing physical force. He is six foot five and weighs 255 pounds. His biceps are "licensed to carry" (i.e., guns), and he has other muscles that barely fit under his gi. He has the overtly masculine ability to be clean-shaven at the morning class and have a full beard by the evening class. Coach has a calm and soothing instructional voice, but there is a tone he can dial into that triggers a fight-or-flight response. It is the tone that most often accompanies the command "move!" Some of my teammates and I haven't forgotten the youngster in the li'l tykes class (ages four to six) being carried out the door by his father, bawling because Coach wouldn't give him a star sticker after class. "You were not paying attention in line, so no star today." Yikes. Can you see why even big-time fighters find him intimidating? I would cry too if I didn't get a star.

Coach started his martial arts training at the age of ten, when he began practicing a style of Karate called Aam-Ka-Jutsu. He studied Aam-Ka-Jutsu for nine years and holds the rank of a first-degree black belt. While watching the UFC, he saw how the use of Jiu-Jitsu skills benefited the most dominant fighters. The athlete who caught his eye was Royce Gracie of the infamous Gracie family. Because BJJ was a rather obscure sport at the time, Coach and some of his equally-as-intrigued Karate black-belt friends, including ToDD, who you will read about later, began to decipher BJJ on their own. Coach recalls his less than enthusiastic Karate master telling him that BJJ was a fad, "just like Kung-Fu was in the '70s. In a couple of years, it'll be gone."

Resources for do-it-yourself Jiu-Jitsu were sparse. Coach and his buddies relied on one book and VHS tapes of Royce Gracie's UFC fights to reverse-engineer what they were seeing into physical maneuvers on the mat. (In contrast, if you google Brazilian Jiu-Jitsu today, you will get 1,440,000 hits.) In compliance with his oft-compulsive behavior, Coach became so obsessed with BJJ that he eventually left the Karate school to study BJJ full-time. He was nineteen. After many years of training and several years of teaching BJJ out of other gyms, Coach opened his own gym location in July 2007.

Fast forward to present day, and Foster Brazilian Jiu-Jitsu has grown to become one of top BJJ schools in the state of Washington, with one of the largest facilities dedicated to the art form.

In addition to teaching, Coach trained as a competitor. Although he has won many medals, he cites his 2006 and 2007 bronze medals from the Pan Jiu-Jitsu Championships, where he competed as a black belt, as major accomplishments.

I'm sure that, along his Jiu-Jitsu journey, Coach has spent time in tutelage of some of the great masters of our day: Mr. Miyagi, Obi-Wan, Gandalf, Professor X, and Homer Simpson all come to mind.

Coach is wise and compassionate. Once (or thrice) when noticing that I was getting watery eyes and on the verge of crumbling, he didn't roll his eyes or ignore me. Instead he looked at me askance with his eyes focused down and to the right, which is the neurolinguistic sign that a person is having an internal dialogue. Without the use of extrasensory perception, I could hear that dialogue as, "Gosh, I've seen that look before. The last time my wife was about to have a breakdown, what did I do that worked?" And I could see his mind churning through his Rolodex of "male responses to irrational female emotions" until he settled on just the right thing to say.

Coach is one of the most genuine people that I know. When you are due a hug, he gives you a real hug, not a lame side-hug. He is a role model for integrity and passion. When he couldn't get what he wanted from BJJ in the area, he took himself elsewhere to train. He returned to generously and enthusiastically share his newly acquired knowledge, just as he does today. He is a student of the art. In his denial of a star sticker to the young Padawan, Coach taught a greater lesson: that you must honor his expectations and the discipline of martial arts. Both coach and learner must not compromise. To practice compromise in the gym will lead you to compromise with yourself in life, and we must always expect to give our best.

Of note, Coach is a self-proclaimed comic-book geek. And thus, the following quote applies: "Just because a guy reads comics, doesn't mean he can't start some shit" (*Mallrats*, 1995).

11

Earning My Stripes

*"To practice any art, no matter how well or badly,
is a way to make your soul grow. So do it."*

— Kurt Vonnegut
A Man Without a Country

There are five ranks in BJJ, and you never know when you will be promoted. Everyone starts off as a white belt or novice. The second rank is a blue belt, followed by purple, brown, and black. In between, you can earn as many as four stripes to signify your progress toward the next belt. A stripe is like getting a gold star by your name. It signifies your commitment and improvement, like little kudos along the way to keep you motivated. How long you stay at any one rank depends entirely on subjective assessment from your instructor. I have seen "naturals" advance from white to purple in less than two years. Likewise, I have seen folks remain a white belt for over three years. There is no set timeline, no scripted agenda—just you, doing your thing to the best of your ability at that time.

On January 27, 2009, I received my first stripe. I had seen other people get stripes, but quite honestly, I did not think I would ever get one. I did not hold my life in high esteem, let alone my rudimentary Jiu-Jitsu. The gym was somewhere I went, not what I was. In my heart, I wasn't committed because my heart was still numb with grief. I liked the challenge of the sport and its novelty, but I thought I was an oddball and that everyone knew I was a phony—a walking lie, pretending I was happy and carefree when inside I always felt as if I was hanging on by a thin thread.

The unpredictability of advancement in Jiu-Jitsu affects people differently. Some people prefer to see the brass ring, have a to-do list to reinforce their competency, and have an actual schedule for paying fees, testing, and getting promoted. These people don't want to be judged; they want to be rewarded. Other people prefer the element of surprise, the ideology that you are expected to work hard and do your best at all times because Coach is always watching. I personally believe Coach was awarded a set of eyes for the back of his head when he earned his black belt.

I don't remember exactly what I felt when Coach called my name, but it was a combination of surprise and "are you sure?" and "someone noticed me?" and then pride—pride that I had stuck with something for three months. I hadn't quit, and someone recognized that. I was so giddy with joy that I took a picture of my stripe with my camera and sent it off to my parents and my brothers and all the people who worried about me. I still use that picture as my icon for the gym's phone number. It remains one of the most significant moments of my life.

That night, I emailed Coach and told him about Carly. I couldn't be a phony anymore if I wasn't invisible. Now Coach would know I was struggling in my personal life. As vulnerable as that made me feel, I also felt a sense of relief. No one at the gym knew me when Carly was alive. They didn't know me as "Carly's mom." I met them when I didn't know who I was anymore. I was still trying to figure it all out. How interesting that the evolution of my progress in Jiu-Jitsu, like my journey through grief, would be, for the most part, a self-directed endeavor, but not a road I would have to walk alone.

12

Cookie Love

I admit to being a food fantasizer.

Today I was thinking that life is a little like having a delightful snack of cookies and milk. Picture a smallish plate loaded (sometimes overloaded) with warm bundles of joy. The milk is the cool, silent partner that waits patiently and predictably within a solid, confident vessel. Life is sweet and conveniently shaped; the anticipation of indulging is like giving yourself a hug. Then, you take that first bite.

Your pearly whites find, perhaps, a little surprise: some cookies are semi-sweet, some you have to chew on for a bit, and some are just plain nutty. Just like life's surprises—that handwritten missive in the mailbox, the chores that get done without asking, the polka-dot panties you find under the Christmas tree.

A smile sneaks onto your face, starting slowly from the corners of your mouth, and you feel a little mischievous, a little celebrated, a little deserving. And you think you have a snug, secure grasp on that piece of life. Not too tight to allow some room for movement, and not too loose to allow for a sense of control. The future looks fantastic; it's a treat.

And then you go for the dunk. It's part of the plan. You knew it was coming—you've been there before, been thinking about it. The dunk enhances the experience, alters the texture, smoothes some edges.

But this time, the plan doesn't go right. During the dunk that cookie falls apart, it falls to a mushy, wet mess at the bottom of your vessel, weighing it down, impossible to put back together. And in your hand, you have the remains of delight, surprise, and joy. There's some there, but it is not the same.

And you stare at what's left and know you are at a crossroads. Are you going to throw the remaining chunk all in, let it all sink to the bottom to sit and clump and stick, soggy fragments, crumbs of life left to pile up at the lowest point?

Just throw it all away, forget it, make it quick. What was once your sweet reward is now a punishment. What did I do to deserve this?

You take another look at what's left. It's not the same. It's smaller, changed, not whole, not as beautiful, and does not provide the same level of joyful anticipation. But it's there, and you hang on to it. You see that parts of it are still sweet, parts still hold surprises. Are you willing to concede that you may find some satisfaction in what's left, even though it's not what you originally had anticipated?

You take a bite of that new life to find out.

13

The Big Easy Roll

T he story of my first year of Jiu-Jitsu would not be complete without my story about New Orleans. I had traveled to New Orleans with my family to vacation over spring break. By no coincidence, I had been there a month prior at a conference and my family was supposed to have joined me, but there was confusion at flight check-in, and it was too late to board by the time they figured things out. So I was on my own in New Orleans for the first trip, and I looked around for and found a Jiu-Jitsu gym in the area, but didn't have time to check it out. During this second trip to New Orleans, I would be able to visit the gym, so it all worked out, right?

My husband and I took the trolley outside the city center and found the Jiu-Jitsu gym. It was a small gym with very friendly staff. I bought a couple of T-shirts, and they invited me back to take a class that evening. I figured we would have family plans, so I didn't really think I would go back. Surprisingly, though, when I asked Chuck what we were doing that night, he said, "Aren't you going to the gym?" *Wow,* I thought, *encouragement?* Chuck and I didn't really talk about my new interest in Jiu-Jitsu; he was just satisfied that it made me happy. "Sure," I said with a smile. So I took a cab and went to roll.

> *"Life is a challenge. Meet it."*
>
> — Mother Theresa

Everyone at the gym was welcoming. They lent me a gi, and I joined right in. The training progression was similar to ours back home: warmup drills, a new technique, and then sparring. Let me mention here that I had told them I was fairly raw: a five-month white belt. I was partnered with a biggish guy, a blue belt, and we began to roll. It was apparent right away that he wasn't going to cut me any slack, so I just tried to ride it out. White belts just survive, right? Well, maybe the philosophy is different down south, because Dude went for the mount and submit. He first tried to armbar me, but my ounce of prevention turned into a pound of wrist-locking, with me on the receiving end. Or maybe it was a pound—or five—of Dude's ego. All I know is that wrists aren't made to bend that far, and we all stopped when we heard the pop. The black belt was sure it was "just a strain," and as a concession, offered to roll with me. Not wanting to be disrespectful or ungrateful, I said yes. But even my high pain threshold has a limit. The second time I rolled over onto my wrist, I had to stop from the pain. The black belt called it a night at the same time—but it wasn't my fault class ended early, right? Don't take it personally—and Dude offered to give me a ride back to my hotel. Sure, we all parted friends.

Back at the hotel room, Chuck wasn't there, and the boys were watching television.

"I think my wrist is broken. I'm gonna get some ice."

"Cool. Hey, Mom, can you bring me a Sprite?"

I walked my pity-party to the hotel bar downstairs and told the bartender my story. He must have felt sorry for me because he put the glass of wine I ordered into a milkshake glass and filled it to the top. He also comped me the Sprite. Back in the room, I sat in the front room of the suite by myself, elevating my arm and staring at the wall. I texted Coach that his goodwill ambassador had her arm broken as a guest roller. He was sympathetic, but I could tell he didn't fully believe me. Later he said that was because I said "arm," not "wrist," and in his infinite BJJ wisdom, he could not fathom how I had gotten a broken arm from a wrist lock. Semantics clouded by pain and cabernet, whatever!

Chuck came back late that night. He seemed surprised to see me still awake and in the front room.

"I think my arm is broken," I said.

Silence, furrowed brow of contemplation. A minute later, "You know, I heard some of the best bands!"

That story of Chuck's reaction still makes me laugh, although I wasn't laughing at the time. We were flying out the next morning, and I wasn't about to go to some suspect Doc-in-the-Box on the fringe of the French Quarter at one a.m. So the next day while we ate beignets and did last minute shopping, I held my arm protectively to my chest and carried on. I even heard, "I'm so glad I married someone who doesn't cry and complain." That's me: warrior wife. I did lose it when the flight attendant bumped into me while handing out cheesy pretzel sticks, but she made up for it with an extra ice bag. Add another page to my Jiu-Jitsu memory book.

> *"I am a warrior. But I'm a girl too."*
>
> — Suki to Sokka, "The Warriors of Kyoshi,"
> *The Last Airbender*

Wait! One more anecdote about the broken wrist. I had to wear a cast, and I chose pink to match my pink gi. At some point, I had decided there was way too much masculinity in the gym and some girl power was necessary, so I'd bought a pink gi. That's also when I got the nickname "Pink." Not very original, but I liked it more than "Cupcake" and "Powder Puff." It's not about who you are; it's what you wear, right? I mean, who really cares who you are? The warrior must always move forward.

When I questioned whether or not I could participate with a cast I heard: "Now your jab will get really good" and "Just don't whack anyone in the head." So I didn't miss a beat. My cast got really nasty-smelling, and I had to have it changed three times. I didn't tell the doctor that I was striking and rolling all the while.

You have to roll creatively when you can only use one hand. One time I was rolling with a BJJ veteran ToDD (a.k.a. Double D, T-Money, Todd-a-licious, Todd the Bod), and I suggested that to make it fair, he should roll with only one hand too. ToDD, not lacking in one bit of confidence, said, "Tell you what, Pink, I won't use any hands." He tucked both of his hands under his belt. Remember I was still a rookie when I tell you that ToDD went on to sweep *and* submit me. ToDD got his black belt a year later.

14

One Numb Duck

One thing I got tired of was everybody telling me how strong I was being, like I was so remarkable. They would say things like: "I could never have gotten through it." "I don't know how you do it."

Do what? Keep living? I didn't feel remarkable. I felt numb. I didn't know what I was doing. I was just trying to survive and make some sense of the world again. Maybe if I were on the outside looking in, I might have said the same things. But I was the one on the inside. Sometimes what I read between the lines was, "Thank God that didn't happen to me."

Did people even comprehend the effort it took for me to get up every day? The effort it took to pretend that I didn't want to curl up and die? The effort it took not to scream: "This is horrible! I'm in pain in my soul. I feel like crap. My life is over. You have no idea what I'm going through." But I never did scream those things, partly because I didn't have the energy and partly because it just isn't my nature. It may have been healthier to vent, to release the intensity of my grief and anger that pushed on my mental and physical boundaries.

One of my coping strategies was my "Be Like A Duck" routine. Ever notice how ducks look so chill on top of the water as they motor around? Yet underneath their stress-free illusion are webbed feet paddling for all they are worth, furiously pushing against the weight of the water. Because I didn't have webbed feet, my furious paddling was hidden inside my mouth, where I had chewed holes in the sides of my cheeks, and in the palms of my hands, where I would dig my nails in until the skin broke.

"Always behave like a duck—keep calm and unruffled on the surface, but paddle like the devil underneath."

— Jacob Braude

15

This Only Happens to Other People

Experiencing a sudden tragedy feels like being a strange place and having the lights go out before you've gotten the lay of the land. For a while you just stand still. Your senses are heightened to the limit of their perception. You see no guidance. Your eyes are useless, and survival is dependent upon deeper senses. You hear no guidance. Your ears strain to go beyond the deep backbeat of your heart pounding. You feel no guidance. Your arms are extended for protection. Tentative steps forward carry anxious precaution. You reach, hoping that you will touch something you recognize, something that will orient you, give you a landmark of your surroundings that feels safe before you feel what you fear most—not knowing. Not knowing if you will trip and fall. Not knowing if you will wander over and over in the same place. The extension of your arms is not only for protection. It also carries with it a sense of longing. Will my reaching out find me the comfort of someone else who shares this same scary place?

Learning to communicate after a loss is like that strange place. So unknown, so full of caution and heightened senses. Everything spoken, or not, has that annoying vocal tilt at the end, the invisible question mark. "Don't hesitate to call?" "Lemme know if you need anything?" "I feel sad?" "I'm doing okay?" "I don't need anything?" "She's in a better place?" "She wouldn't want you to feel that way?" It's true that most people don't know what to say. But now I do. I've been on the receiving end more than anyone should ever have to endure. Plenty of people would have been better off not saying anything to me. At some point, I learned to just nod, realizing that at times, it was more about them feeling better.

And communicating within your own family is the most difficult. That is the darkest-of-dark strange places. You don't fear bumping into the elephant in the room. You fear that it takes up all the space and breathes all the oxygen and will squish you against the wall when you acknowledge it. And you know you need to talk about it, but you can't. In one way, it feels like not talking out of respect for the "everyone grieves differently" adage. And in another way, it feels like not talking because you don't know how. I'm from a family of talkers. I grew up with each of us talking about our day at the dinner table and the freedom to ask questions of the speaker. We asked "why," "how," and "what happened next?" Maybe I married a quiet guy to get away from all that inquisition. Chuck operates under the mindset of "if they want to tell me, they will." He is not nosy or pushy; he is pensive and reflective—always. I am pensive and reflective only after I have reached peak emotional output. He says I talk enough for the both of us, so he just listens. When he does talk, his words are thoughtful and intelligent. They always mean something.

After Carly died, it was hard to talk. There might be a thousand reasons why that could have applied at any given time. I didn't talk at first because I was almost always crying. I think that is why no one else talked, because if I wasn't crying, they feared that what they were going to say would trigger another shower of tears. We didn't talk because we were all in pain. When you are hurting badly, you go into personal survival mode, not caretaker mode. I remember talking to Kathleen about this in one of our earlier sessions. When I really thought about it, not talking in our house—although I understood why we weren't—made me lonely. But as soon as Kathleen offered up, "Why don't you coach Chuck and the boys on how to—," I cut her off. "No. Look, I can barely take care of myself right now. I do not have the emotional energy to teach someone else how to talk to me." I felt like saying, "They should all just get up and go to counseling too."

And maybe they should have gone to counseling. I wasn't going to force it on anyone. Chuck and the boys did go see Kathleen once with me. The boys, who were thirteen and ten at the time, said very little. I remember Eason putting his head way down inside his hoodie and pulling the strings so we couldn't see him. Carson lay across my lap and just shrugged his shoulders whenever Kathleen asked him a question. I did learn a lot about how Chuck was feeling, though. Somehow it was easier for him to talk to a third person in front of me than it was to talk to me in front of me. I get that. What most people don't know is that Chuck's mom had died the day before Carly had. Any grieving to take place for Mary, Gramma May-May, got put on hold.

Chuck's mom had a stroke that left her debilitated and in the hospital for a couple of weeks. Things were touch-and-go and not looking good when Carly and I left for North Carolina. The kids knew that Gramma was in the hospital, but I'm not sure they comprehended that she might not ever come back out of it. Mary was the absolute salt-of-the-earth person. From the day I met her, I never heard her utter a negative word about anyone. She was the Gramma who would let you eat Cheetos and drink soda at ten a.m. in her recliner and who would play endless rounds of Clue and Uno.

Carly was old enough to know that Mary's condition was grave and constantly asked for updates. Chuck called me around east coast dinnertime to tell me that his mom had passed away. We were eating what would be our last team dinner. The look on my face must have told Carly something was up, and she asked about Gramma. I froze up. I didn't know what to tell her. I didn't know if we should fly back home or play the tournament. If we stayed, would she be able to play if she was upset about Mary? So I just said, "She is hanging in there," figuring I would let it all gel and deal with it the next day.

Later that night, which would be early in the morning the next day, Chuck and I lost our daughter too. I believe as strongly as I have ever believed anything that Mary died right before Carly so that she could be there waiting for her when she arrived. She would be there so that Carly wouldn't be scared. She would be there to hold her, welcome her, and tell her everything was going to be okay. And that comforts me. It comforts me, although I want to be the one to hold her and tell her everything is going to be okay. And that thought puts me in the strange, dark place again . . . my arms extended with longing, reaching for one more hug that I can't find.

Did we all eventually learn to communicate better? I think we learned to communicate in a way that worked for us. When we weren't communicating at first as a family, I found other people to communicate with—friends mostly; sometimes people who attached themselves to me, then left; but no group meetings, which never appealed to me. Perhaps I spent too much time with them talking, crying, and sharing stories about Carly. It was a while before I learned that this was distancing me from my family. I think I sought out these people out because they were emotionally available and felt safe. They were hurting too, but in my mind, could never hurt with the same deep pain I was—the pain that comes with losing someone you have watched grow up, shared a home with, and experienced the gamut of emotions with, in the way only a parent or sibling can. My older brother said, "I can't believe it. This is what happens to other people, something you read about in the paper." I guess I am "other people" now. My younger brother couldn't be near me at Carly's memorial. It was just too hard for him to see me. He didn't know what to say. He himself was devastated and trying to learn to communicate. He was in survival mode. No excuses, no blame, no what-if, no if-only, no going back.

I have learned from Chuck to be more pensive and reflective. I can understand that I did—we all did—what we had to do to navigate a dark and scary place. And in the end we found each other, and we found a way out.

16

Takedowns, Breakdowns

*"Pain is the breaking of the shell
that encloses your understanding."*

— Kahlil Gibran

I look back on my journey, and I wonder if part of the reason I stuck with Jiu-Jitsu was because it allowed me to feel again. Before I started training, I did all kinds of things to numb myself from the emotional pain. Today I can tell you that numbing the pain only makes it worse when you finally feel it. Before Jiu-Jitsu, I did my share of not-so-positive things, trying to feel good again, to feel anything again, to see if there was part of me left somewhere. With Jiu-Jitsu, I found myself not only feeling again, but feeling plenty.

Much of that feeling came from the pain of takedowns class. I started going to this particular class because I didn't know anything about it (curiosity can kill a cat here), and that particular night was one I had free. How bad could it be? I hated takedowns class pretty much right from the first clinch and head drag. Okay, hate is a strong word: I had great dislike for takedowns class. But I still went. It was at this class that I broke three toes (my own), got the wind knocked out of me several times, and once was covered with so many bruises my massage therapist stopped counting and called Child Protective Services. (Just kidding!) Once a guy with a Judo background threw me down seven (7!) times in a row, each time right after I got up from the last time. Not a lot of people did the takedowns class, and I could see why.

> *"The greatest glory in living lies not in never falling, but in rising every time we fall."*
>
> — Nelson Mandela

I did takedowns class for about one and a half years . . . until they started a Women's BJJ and Self-Defense class the same night, and I had to stick up for the other ovaries in the gym. I know that I know a lot of takedowns—more than several of the guys at the gym, but I don't execute them very well in competition. That is a different matter all together.

I can now admit that one of the initial reasons I stuck with takedowns was for the pain, as sick as that sounds. Physical pain is nothing compared to emotional pain. If I was aching, then I was alive, right? I would be so sore I couldn't roll over in bed, so sore the bottoms of my feet would hurt. Places I didn't know could hurt would hurt. But I would just sort of smile as I limped and groaned along my merry way. In class, people are throwing you to the mat every which way from Sunday, and even though they taught me how to fall, I resembled Humpty Dumpty in falling ability. And I still went back. I didn't realize it then, but I had turned a corner and faced my fears by taking on the challenge of that class. Maybe it was because it gave me a sense of accomplishment to go—even though I never really wanted to be there—to tell myself, "You did it again. You got through." That class scared me. My husband would be shaking his head every time I left the house or showed him a new injury. Somehow he must have known that I thought I needed this. It's that warrior-wife thing again.

17

The Choke

B efore I started training at Jiu-Jitsu, my idea of choking was something you did on a hotdog, requiring the Heimlich maneuver. In Jiu-Jitsu, choking your opponent is one way to get him to submit. There are all kinds of chokes: baseball choke, collar choke, Ezekial choke, Darce choke, paper cutter choke; chokes using the lapel of the gi; chokes that use the gi skirt; and who knows, probably the belt too. There are blood chokes that make you pass out because they press on the carotid arteries, soft-tissue chokes, and airway chokes. Sometimes you don't feel like you are being choked; it just hurts, so you tap.

One of my vivid memories of choking took place early in my training. During one of the sparring sessions, I was partnered with T, a nice guy often referred to as "The Energizer Bunny" because he had the frightening ability to go at a wicked speed for a very long time. I don't remember the speed as much as I remember him trying to choke me from behind for a very long time. I do remember trying to fend him off and hang on until the timer went off . . . probably two minutes, but it felt like twenty. When the timer beeped, he let go, said "Good job," and moved on to find another victim. I, on the other hand, had been shaking so badly I went into the lobby to compose myself.

At some point, Coach came out and sat beside me. "Are you okay?"

In between breaths of hyperventilation, I replied, "He . . . was . . . trying to . . . choke . . . . me really . . . hard." I'm sure that Coach was half-laughing, but I wouldn't look him in the eye to find out. "Well," he continued, "now when you compete, you will know how it really feels, and you'll be ready. You are feeling all that adrenaline and the adrenaline dump."

I didn't know what an adrenaline dump was, but I barely heard anything after he said, "Now when you compete . . ."

What? I was thinking, *Are you nuts? I'm not even sure I think this is fun.* All that came out my mouth, however, was: "Yeah, sure."

I learned later that an adrenaline dump is the aftereffect of a big adrenaline rush. The adrenaline rushes in to prep you for "fight or flight." Afterward, if you haven't learned to control the rush, you will feel an overwhelming fatigue as the adrenaline leaves the bloodstream. It felt more like posttraumatic stress disorder to me.

Besides being choked literally, a person can choke figuratively. In athletics, this can be described as a loss of confidence, an inability to move, an increase in anxiety, loss of emotional control, and waves of doubt. Interestingly, I was suffering all of those symptoms as I learned to cope with grief. I had lost my focus. I engaged in negative self-talk that led to surges of anxiety. My anxiety made it difficult to breathe fluidly or be calm, left me nervous, weak, and shaky. In sports, choking is fairly unpredictable, which makes it so scary. If you've choked once, you are never sure when you will choke again.

My form of choking—choking on life—was rather predictable, but it was still very scary because I couldn't control it. Would I ever be able to put myself on the line—or on the mat? When you choke, it's embarrassing. You feel guilty, that you have let everyone down. I can see now how I let these feelings (the fear of choking on my grief) rob me of my motivation to move forward in my life.

Grief chokes you just like I was being choked on the mat by my training partner. Over time, I have learned to apply the survival tactics from the mat to my life. You have to hang on as long as you can because in life you do not know when the timer will go off. Be present. Embrace the rush of adrenaline and control it. Think about what is happening now, not about what might happen later or what just happened. Manage your energy so you can maintain it at a constant level. Control your breathing by slowing it down. You have to relax and reduce muscle tension, allowing your ribs to expand and let the air in. Lastly, turn up the volume on positive self-talk.

Employing all of these strategies takes practice. I have learned to be gentler with myself when I deviate from positive practice. And I have learned some defenses when the choke comes on hard. Grief is a battle. Fight to win—don't fight not to lose.

18

Stay Connected
to the Earth

C oach has a resonant way of saying "stay connected to the Earth." On the mat, it means to keep at least one foot planted firmly on the mat so that you always have a physical focal point from which to push off. If I do not have a foot securely on the Earth, I will not be able to leverage my opponent. This is analogous to staying emotionally grounded. You must be whole and present. In Jiu-Jitsu, if you let your mind wander, if you are not fully present in your body, your opponent will have his arm around your neck, and if you do not become present and tap out, you will become unconscious and pass out.

In life, we seek to be grounded in physical, spiritual, mental, and emotional well-being. Many of us are stuck in the paradigm of entitlement. I know I was. Before Carly died, I felt entitled to her—indeed, my own—well-planned future. I felt entitled to my emotional and spiritual security. I felt entitled to my health and intellect. And I felt entitled to knowing when my life was going to change so that I could prepare. But we are not entitled to these types of groundedness. We have to work for them.

One of the hardest things for me to accept about Jiu-Jitsu was that I had no control over what my opponent might do. In my mind, I would formulate brilliant game plans for sparring and competition. I would visualize the entire session. Then in reality, my opponent wouldn't follow my brilliant plan, and I would be lost. Often I would freeze up or fall a step behind while trying to make a new plan in real time. I wasn't able to adapt and flow without great effort. I would get angry with myself, and sometimes, with my opponent. I would lose my groundedness. Now when I am sparring and tactics go awry, the first thing I ask myself—after *are you remembering to breathe?*—is *are you connected to the Earth?* I know that if I can get at least one foot firmly on the mat, then I will find the leverage to upset my opponent and regain my sense of well-being. When my opponent is Grief, and I fear its tight grip around my neck, I also ask myself if I am connected to the Earth. Life requires that we are consummately receptive, regardless of preparation. We must adapt and flow seamlessly. Being connected to the Earth provides the comfort I need to get closer to my grief.

Accommodating grief and fear takes courage. Early on, I believed that I could not do it. I could not accept that my daughter was gone. Every day I had to decide whether or not I had the courage to face the day and thinking that I might be overwhelmed by emptiness and give up. For a long time, I was far from grounded. Time is the enemy of grief, and I eventually learned to live with the feelings of uncertainty grief left for me. I can't say that I embraced those feelings or anything that enlightened, but I did learn to carry them with me as if they were a wild animal in a small cage. I felt empowered that I could bring them under my control, knowing that at any given moment, I had the power to release them. That release would only happen when I allowed it, when I felt equipped to face those feelings, brave enough to retrain my response to fear so that its hold on me was not as strong and crippling.

Will we ever become allies, grief and I? I think it's possible we may have a commensal coexistence, like tolerant roommates. Do I respect the power of grief? Absolutely. But that does not mean I have to play the subservient role. I also do not have to define my grief and fear as good or bad, and instead simply see them as they are. I don't have to try to escape from them. In the past, when I tried to escape from my grief, I sought comfort externally. (Cue the choirboys singing "Looking for Love in all the Wrong Places.") If I ate, drank, bought, watched, or read "this," I would feel better. I was my own worst counselor, thinking that all of these external things would make me feel better, but instead made me feel worse. The affirmation I sought was short-lived, and

I would suffer from an "emotional hangover." These hangovers left me drained, cloudy-headed, irritable, bloated, angry, and steeped in pathos. I was disconnected from the Earth.

Like an addiction, I kept participating in these disconnecting behaviors. You know how, when you were little, you would come home and say "Mom, my [body part] hurts when I do this . . ." And Mom, gifted with maternal wisdom, would say, "Then don't do that." That's how self-destruction tortures you. You engage in the self-destructive behavior because there is a period of time where you don't see your behavior as self-destructive; you see it as comforting and a portal to a better time. Then comes a time when you know your behavior is self-destructive. You then have to decide if you are going to engage in that behavior. Sometimes you do engage, because you feel like you deserve to feel shitty. Other times, you can resist and tell yourself that, maybe if you don't feel shitty about yourself, you can feel better about everything else . . . like being able to see Carly's picture or walk past her room, and to respond with memories that make me smile and give me a sense of thankfulness for what I had with her, not what I am missing now.

—◆—

That's my journey. I'm not there. But I do feel like I'm on my way. Sort of like Dorothy and her yellow brick road. Hers was not an easy road to follow. There were flying monkeys, intoxicating flowers, and an evil witch trying to keep her down. But Dorothy was resilient, wasn't she? I'm not going to braid my hair and wear a pinafore, but like Dorothy, I am going to surround myself with friends who can help me stay on the road. I am going to fight back. I may not get what I want the first time—remember how Dorothy got turned away at the gate?—but I am integrating the strength and tools I need to live fully my life as it is now. I will stay connected to the Earth.

> "And the day came when the risk to remain tight in a bud
> was more painful than the risk it took to blossom."
>
> — Anais Nin

19

Biochemistry

I f part of groundedness involves taking care of your physical, inside self, then I was a wreck. Sure, I was getting exercise now; I had integrated back into society, work, friends, etc., but physically I felt terribly unbalanced. I had been training at Jiu-Jitsu for about six months, even competed one time. But I did not feel like an athlete. I was still heavy. I would get gassed during training. My weight would fluctuate five or ten pounds constantly. I was pre-hypertensive. The blood pressure really freaked me out because I had been 110/70 my whole life. I was tired, frustrated, and stressed out.

Again, a power beyond random chance intervened. During the fundraiser for The Carly Stowell Foundation I mentioned previously (see Chapter 7), a last-minute donation was added to our silent auction. It was for a full wellness evaluation with a naturopath. I had always been curious about naturopathy, and it was obvious to me that my traditional Western tactics were failing. I bid and I "won." (I think it's funny when we are at silent auctions that my kids think we "won" something. *Uh, no honey, that's not how it works.*) I met Lisa two months after the fundraiser and following the holidays, and I felt at my physical rock bottom.

Naturopathic medicine is different from conventional medicine. The fundamental tenets of the practice reflect on treating the whole person with a holistic approach. It supports the innate ability our bodies have to heal themselves with the support of ancient healing wisdom and modern scientific knowledge. Lisa has an undergraduate degree in cell and molecular biology and a naturopathic doctorate degree. Because I also had a background in the sciences and did my graduate work in molecular biology, we were able to "speak the same language." Identifying and treating the underlying cause of any imbalance requires knowledge of both physiologic and nutritional biochemistry, endocrinology (hormones), and the science behind emotional health. It isn't "hocus-pocus," as my dad first called it. Later he conceded that whatever it was, naturopathy was certainly working for me and was therefore acceptable.

Lisa empowered and educated me to not only move toward wellness but to manage and maintain it. On her website is this most applicable tenet: "I endeavor to educate you how to care for yourself, and in turn you can help others care for themselves."

Lisa confirmed some things I knew: my blood pressure was high, I was anemic, I was fat (she didn't say it like that), my blood chemistry was a disaster, and I was spiritually wiped out. What I didn't know was that my adrenal glands had been impacted by my chronic intense stress and my cortisol release was actually backwards from normal. These factors were likely the reason my weight kept changing and I had no energy. She patiently listened to my story of how I had gotten to this place, never judging, rushing, or blaming me. This is in stark contrast to some medical doctors, who, with little time and lots of patients, just looked at your chart, gave you a prescription, and said "adios" after fifteen minutes. Lisa was the most refreshing intervention I'd received.

I think it was no coincidence that I ended up in Lisa's office. When I saw her writing some things down, I gasped in shock, "You hold your pencil just like Carly." My daughter had a bizarre way of holding her pencil that would have driven parochial school nuns crazy. It drove me crazy because I was subjected to nun-like penmanship and Pencil-Holding 101 back in elementary school. Carly held her pencil between her index and middle fingers and used her middle finger to press down on the pencil. I had never seen that style before, not even in any of my students during the course of my teaching career. To see that Lisa held her pencil the same way was a sign to me that I was supposed to be there and that I could trust her to help me unconditionally.

And help me she did. Let me be the first to say, though, that I did the hard work. She counseled and made suggestions and did the tests, but I was the one who gagged down some nasty-tasting supplements and followed through on her regimens. It was baby steps. And I didn't agree to everything. I adamantly refused to give up coffee for a long time. I didn't find "mindful time" every day. But I did honor the process. When I said I would do something, I did. And I started to see results. I didn't lose weight for a while, but I did get smaller, more toned. I definitely saw a change in my energy level, and I slept better. I began to feel like I could think more clearly.

When Lisa suggested something, she would also explain why she was suggesting it. She knew that I was a science person so she always included the biochemistry behind the nutritional suggestions, and I always got to see my laboratory results. There is a part of me that responds best to the numbers—the facts that drive the reality home. Lisa reinforced many things about nutrition that I knew, but had only dabbled in and certainly had not participated in for over a year. I had come to the point where I had nothing to lose (but weight), so I listened to everything she said.

Naturally, my improved health was a plus on the mat. I felt more energized and had more stamina. I had a more positive outlook about myself and my future. I learned that the choices I had been making to comfort myself were not healthy choices, and they affected how I competed. When I felt pressured, my Old Self would grab a bottle of wine and some Oreo's and hit the couch. I learned to ask myself, "Do you really want to do this? You know how you will feel tomorrow. Is it worth it?" With this new attitude, Lisa helped me hone my nutritional plan while I trained for Worlds. Yes, beet juice does help build endurance. And mentally, Lisa taught me how to relax my mind. We talked about my goals: how I had always wanted to have a plan, but did not want to become obsessive about it. I had been directionless for long time. When I would finally decide to do something, I had always given it up after a couple of weeks—except the Jiu-Jitsu.

So I admitted to Lisa that I was afraid, afraid that too much focus on any one thing would bring back my stress. I no longer wanted to ride an aimless wave; however, I wanted goals to be my guide and to allow myself permission to waiver occasionally. I wanted to be well, but I didn't want the process to control my life. I didn't need any more stress.

Lisa taught me that FEAR is "Forgetting Everything is All Right."

> *"We see the world not as it is, but as we are."*
>
> — The Talmud

My work with Lisa also taught me to be more patient and present with others. It was hard for me to be patient and present when my modus operandi had become give-up, breakdown, self-destruct, and feel guilty about it. I learned not to react impulsively to protect myself. Instead, I learned to slow down, breathe, and think about the consequences of my choices. I listen more intentionally. I accept that everyone has a different context from which they are operating.

For a long time, I did not see the world as a place I wanted to be in because I didn't think the world wanted me in my grieving state. Now I try to consider that whatever it is that people are saying or doing stems from roots we cannot possibly see, from something deep inside them with which they are struggling. Sometimes we *do* because we cannot *say*, and sometimes we *say* because we cannot *do*. Life is not an exam with only one way to solve the problem. Everybody's problem is different, and everybody's route to the answer is different.

20

Toleration

With Lisa, my internal healing wasn't all about biochemistry. It also involved controlling my stress and anxiety so that I could level my emotional playing field. One way that we worked on this was through an exercise where you reduce your "tolerations."

Tolerations are any and all of those things, people, activities, etc., that create a drag on your time and energy. A toleration is tradeoff of some kind, and you may realize during this exercise that the trade is not a good one for you or possibly that it is more than good enough.

We tolerate some things because our return on the investment is wonderful, if not reasonable. But those things that we tolerate because we think we should or because we don't want to rock the boat, those are the tolerations that can drain us of our life force. Those tolerations become obstacles to having a more simple, straightforward life. In fact, Lisa proffers that many tolerations are the very things that make adults so exhausted, suppressed, and high-strung. Lisa credits Personal Coach Thomas Leonard with the exercise.

To get started, I find a quiet place to be alone with my thoughts, a pen, some paper, and a timer (this is a very important apparatus).

Then I set the timer for two minutes and write down a list of all things I tolerate—nothing is off limits. You only get two minutes, or else you might write for hours and never get to the second part of the exercise. The tolerations you think of first probably are those closest to the surface and most poignant anyway. After two minutes, you are supposed to walk away. Give your list some time to gel before part two.

Part two is a cost-benefit analysis. Look at each toleration and be honest about what it is costing you to tolerate it. Write this down. Likewise, any benefits of the toleration should be recorded. Then, again walk away.

I am a big proponent of the walk-away factor. If I get too wrapped up in an emotional task, I cannot be as objective about it as I would like.

When I return to the list, then I do my analysis of the whole. This usually makes me pause and say, "Dang, I've used up a lot of emotional energy lately." The whole experience is quite an eye-opener.

I then decide which tolerations I am willing to accept. This involves eliminating those things I tolerate because I really have no control over them. In realizing that I cannot control certain aspects of my life, I also know that I do have control over how I respond to these aspects. I have the choice to let them pain me, like a pinch of salt on an open wound, or I can shrug it off with or without a band-aid of consideration. Letting go of the things I tolerate but can't control frees up my emotional energy to deal with things I can control.

As I look at my list, I decide if the cost of the toleration is worth it or not. Costs are like lead weights holding me down. Benefits are like removing the weight. They are what you will gain from letting the toleration go.

I measure the costs and benefits of tolerating these things in my life, and then I make a plan of change. It is up to me to follow through with that plan. Sometimes I follow through and sometimes I don't. Sometimes the same toleration comes up over and over again because I can't rally myself to face it head on. But at least I have given it a name and an acknowledgment. I have given myself a place to start.

The success in this exercise is that, when you recognize the weight behind each cost and benefit, you will create some better choices for yourself. Some of those choices will include a plan for change: a plan for dealing with the toleration that will reduce its cost. For example, my jeans don't fit—again—and yet I continue to keep them and tolerate how it makes me feel every time I try them on. There are different plans for change that I can choose from: I can get rid of the jeans, I can find a gym, I can commit to walk every day, or I can buy a bigger size. I need to decide if not dealing with the toleration is costing me more than ignoring it. I decide that I will feel better not having the jeans as a reminder, so I get rid of the jeans and the weight of that toleration.

The cost of any toleration is usually, but not always, at the emotional level. Take, for instance, the coworker who talks behind your back. You put up with it because you don't want to confront her about how you feel, though you realize her actions cause you to distrust her. You don't want to confide in her because you are sure it will come back to bite you, so instead you keep quiet, possibly becoming resentful, so much so that you no longer enjoy your workspace. When you recognize that the benefit of not confronting her (the stress of confrontation) actually outweighs the cost of not being able to enjoy your work environment as much or to speak as freely as you'd like, you will be able to create better choices for yourself in this scenario. For example, you would surround yourself with trusted colleagues, or perhaps you would find a way to get to know her better. The cost of continuing to tolerate your coworker's backstabbing behavior is a tradeoff that you endorse because of the greater weight of the fear and stress it would cause you to confront her.

After a few runs through this exercise, I began to notice a similar theme to the tolerations on my list: I said yes when I really wanted to say no. After reflecting on this, I was able to admit that too often I weigh the cost to the other person as being of greater importance than the cost to myself. Saying yes when you want to say no comes up often when you are grieving. People invite you places and want to take care of you. You let them say things that irritate you, and you attend events you don't want to attend. I did this at first because I was numb, and it was easy to be led around and cared for. I also did this because

I wanted to avoid confrontation. Later, as I started to stand on my own a little stronger, I was able to understand that I was saying yes when I wanted to say no because I knew it made people feel good, and I didn't want them to feel bad. I already felt blue; I didn't want to be the sadness propagator. So I tolerated this behavior in myself over and over again, until I started to resent the people who tried to help.

My toleration lists also contain BJJ tolerations. Sometimes I tolerate a training partner with bad breath. I realize that next time I might be the one who smells like the Puget Sound at low tide. The risk of embarrassing a teammate is a greater cost to me than practicing my self-assertion skills.

I long ago learned to tolerate that BJJ will ruin my pedicure. No matter how dry the polish, the kneeling will wear the polish off the tip of my nail every time. Instead of being exacerbated, I now call it my "BJJ French Tip" and think maybe I'll be a trendsetter.

When I started rolling, it bothered me that I didn't ask questions when I had them, yet I kept doing it. I felt too intimidated to ask questions, and then I would go home frustrated that I was still confused or didn't get the help I needed. Ironically, in my classroom one day, I caught myself saying to a student, "Just ask. There are probably many students here with the same question." Hmm . . . what a hypocrite I was! But now, since I have acknowledged the toleration, I could work to fix it, and I did.

What did it cost me? Perhaps a little embarrassment at first.

What did I gain? The satisfaction of an answer, relief from frustration, and the sense that I honored my feelings.

Most of us would be amazed at the number of things we tolerate every day—things that we could can change, some very easily, with just a little communication or a little bit of time. Sure there are times when the investment is too high, and we choose instead to "just tolerate." But most of the time, if we are willing to make the investment to unhinge the intolerable by dealing with it directly, we can move forward in our lives with a much lighter stress load.

21

Just Breathe

"Life's ups and downs provide windows of opportunity to determine your values and goals. Think of using all obstacles as stepping stones to build the life you want."

— Marsha Sinetar

D uring the fall of 2010, I had decided that I wanted to focus on Jiu-Jitsu and myself. Before then, but since Carly's death, I had focused on lots of other peoples' kids through coaching and the sponsored activities of the nonprofit foundation we had started in her name. I had also decided that I would not return as a club volleyball coach. The club season, practices, and tournaments interfered with my competition team practice at Foster's. I didn't want to give that up.

Then I got some news that did not support my decision. In December 2010, I saw a doctor about a medical issue, who recommended that I give up any sort of weightlifting and Jiu-Jitsu and to have a fairly major surgery. After surgery, I would not be able to return to these activities because, in his opinion, they were exacerbating my condition, and so, if I did not stop after surgery, I would suffer recurrences. I was devastated. I tried to explain how Jiu-Jitsu had become integral to my newfound health and well-being. He seemed nonplussed and encouraged me to schedule the surgery for the summer. Holding back tears, I said that I would get a second opinion and try some more conservative therapies.

I spent a great deal of my winter break in pensive contemplation. And I stood firm on my original decision. I was not going to give up Jiu-Jitsu. I would go to the physical therapy appointments the doctor recommended, and I would teach myself to do things differently so I wouldn't make the condition worse.

The physical therapy sucked—too much time doing exercises I could easily do on my own time in my own home. Three weeks of that and I was ready to move on. I knew that what I needed to do was strengthen my core and learn to breathe differently. When you have what is essentially a hernia, you can't hold your breath when you exert yourself. When I returned from my holiday, I did three things. First, I found a trainer in the area who would help me with my breathing. Second, I committed myself to core work. Last, I called the surgeon and said, "No, thank you." Whew, huge step. A year ago I would have felt sorry for myself and given in. I would have thought that I don't matter so why would something I wanted matter? When something horrible happens in your life, there's this part of you that thinks you deserve more bad things to happen because life already has you down. It's easier for life to keep picking on you than to start on some fresh, strong person. At least it seemed that way sometimes. Lots of times.

I started working with JoAnn on my breathing. JoAnn is a member of a small but special group of people I like to call my Wellness Team. They are people I met along my journey who helped keep me in one piece, and they represent many fields of expertise. JoAnn is a retired ex-sky goddess turned personal trainer, massage therapist, Pilates instructor, and manual ligament therapy practitioner. She lives ten minutes from my house so she is convenient assistance. Dr. Z is a sports-centered chiropractor who was my rehab man after my shoulder froze and I had my wrist broken. Like Chuck, he shakes his head in wonderment when I arrive a bit banged up, but he never stops encouraging me. If I am the rusty Tin Man, then Dr. Z is the guy who picks up my oil can—my tune-up man. Lastly, there is Louise, an Ashi massage therapist who works on Coach and Brick. I figured that if she can handle those big guys, then I'm a walk in the park, and I mean that literally: an Ashi massage therapist walks on your back and uses her body weight to dig into those tight and sore spots.

Okay, so I went to JoAnn for breathing lessons. I know you are snickering. I realize the thought of "breathing lessons" sounds silly, but I worked hard at it, and I saw results. JoAnn would put me into some challenging positions—for example, a reverse plank with a ball on my stomach that wasn't supposed to fall off as I inhaled and exhaled for so many counts. These moves worked my core, and I would have to time and control my breath as I moved from one position to another. Initially, I found it very difficult. I had been practicing bad breathing for most of my athletic life. That's probably why the prescription to calm myself down through breathing never really worked for me.

Before breathing training, on the mat, my breathing had been the butt of many a carping critique. At first I was instructed to simply stop holding my breath, because I would do this while I executed moves or had to scramble. I didn't even know I was doing it. I heard that my lips would turn blue. Looking back, I can compare then and now. When I started I was such a spaz that it was all I could do to figure out where all my limbs were and tell my left from my right. I kid you not—turn yourself upside down and have someone yell, "Move your left hip out to the right and take your right arm and reach your opponent's left pant leg . . ." C'mon, that part is still hard. Anyway, can you see how adding "remember to breathe" can get lost in the shuffle?

My work with JoAnn and my subsequent improvement of Jiu-Jitsu skills eventually led to better breathing. Better, not great. I have always disliked breathing through my nose, but I concur that it does help to slow your breathing down. Sadly, I never feel like I can get as much air through two little holes in my perky little nose as I can through the large aperture of my mouth. My compromise to the commands of "Breathe! Breathe through your nose!" had always been to breathe through my mouth. The problem with doing that: discretion is tricky. Let's just say that everyone always knew where I was rolling.

The carping shifted to, "Quiet your breathing."

"At least you know I am breathing!" was my reply.

Since then, I have made great strides in the breathing arena. I have learned that when I am confident and in better shape, I can focus on quiet, controlled breathing and not be a spaz. Breathing is a skill that athletes must consider seriously for optimum performance.

Breathing is also a useful tool off the mat. I tell myself to breathe when I feel that I am going to think myself into a panic attack. I tell myself to breathe before I react to things people say that upset me. I tell myself to breathe when I need to quiet my mind and reconnect to the Earth. It does take practice!

I still have trouble telling my left from my right while upside down, but now I don't turn blue as I'm figuring it out.

Photo by Kim Walker.

Somebody stop me!

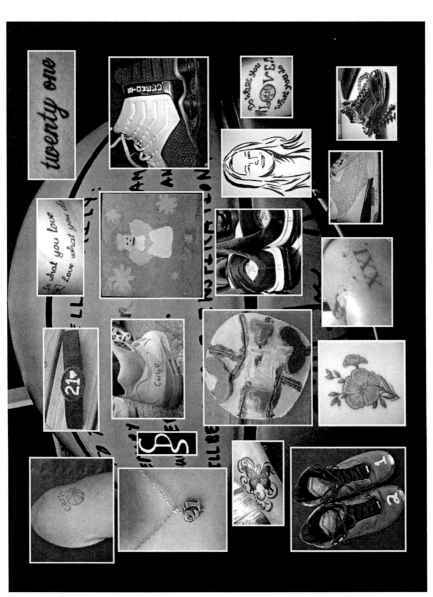

Carly tribute tattoos from left to right: Mike, Cody, Chanel, Kendall, Elena, Cynthiann, Morganne (collage by Mike Baltierra).

California cousins, Christmas 2006.

Christmas 2006.

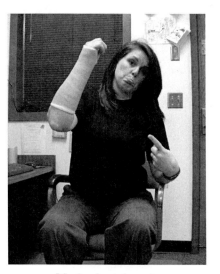

My fresh pink cast.

Looking determined at striking class.

ToDD teaching me a guard
pass lesson.

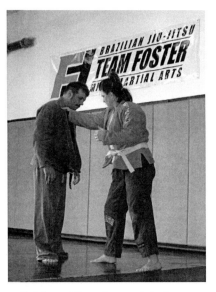

Brick and I work on a takedown.

A love of music begins

Carly and Kendall duet (photo by Kim Walker).

Carly's first hot tub at three months old.

Eason and Carson. The whole family loves hoops!

Me and some of the coaching staff: Brick, Jeff B, Coach, ToDD, Bobi, Jimmie
(photo by Mike Baltierra).

Coach passing Brick's half-guard (photo by Mike Baltierra).

Carly with Morganne and Cody in the chapel at Duke (photo by Quentin Sisco).

It's impossible to keep Coach in side
control (photo by Mike Baltierra).

Training with Jean, a black belt from
Brazil (photo by Mike Baltierra).

Brick is always ready to hold
the harness (photo by Mike
Baltierra).

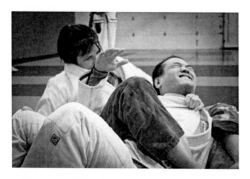

Catching Ed "The Champ" in a bow and
arrow choke (photo by Mike Baltierra).

Team Foster. From left to right: back row: Bobi, Nicole, Carlos, Matt, Jason, Tunz, Brick, Big Mike; front row: Kevin, Josh, Coach, Jimmie, Jean, Me, Stuart (photo by Mike Baltierra).

22

Celebrate Small Victories

I can remember the exact moment when Coach first said this to me: celebrate small victories. He was making light of an interchange between Brick and me, where I was certain that I was correctly describing a takedown to a teammate, and that Brick was confused. I went and asked Coach if I was right. And I was right! I was ha-ha-ing Brick *neener-neener* (in a most respectful way, because he is a coach) when Coach said, "You have to celebrate small victories." Yes, I do. Dang straight! And especially in this instance, because it was the first time I had enough confidence with a technique to stick up for myself.

From that day forward, *celebrate small victories* became a mantra of mine. While I was training for Worlds, I had many a practice where I felt like I wasn't doing anything right. There was one practice where I was so frustrated, I took off my belt and threw it down because I wanted to leave (i.e., go cry). To this day I feel guilty about throwing my belt—it's sacrilegious—but Brick was holding the harness patiently waiting for me to strap in and do my sprints. Coach yelled over, "If you are frustrated, take it out on the sprints." Beating myself up was not productive, and no one was going to let me get away with it. When you run the harness you have to think of other things because it's hard work: your legs burn and your lungs scream. After spending the first laps thinking about how pissed I was, I started to think about small victories. If I couldn't find one in my Jiu-Jitsu, maybe I could find one in my effort. I was running the harness—no one else was waiting to take a run. I could do it; my victory was that I was working hard. I was working hard, even though I had performed poorly at practice. And you know what? I actually started to smile during that harness session. My small victory lifted my spirits and changed my attitude.

After each practice, I made myself find one small victory to celebrate. Some days when I really got my ass kicked, my victory might be, "I got out of the *first* armbar" or "I didn't give up (the whole time I was being pummeled)," or "It's not as swollen as last time." Eventually I was able to find small victories in "I got my sweep on so-n-so" and "I didn't get caught in that choke today (which I got caught in yesterday)."

Celebrate small victories. It was amazing to me how three little words could change my outlook. They helped me to focus on the things that I was doing right instead of the things I thought I was doing wrong. I became able to reframe how I evaluated my performance at practice. By doing this, I began to get more out of my practices.

I also began to use that mantra off the mat. If I was discouraged at work, or was letting my negative sad-self take over, I would stop, breathe, and ask, "What's your small victory today?" I could always find one, which would turn my frown upside down.

My own children and students have heard me ask them about their small victories. Carson was trying out for the high school golf team and felt that during tryouts he played the worst golf ever. All he could tell me about were his mistakes. So I let him vent and then I said, "You need to find a small victory every day. Tell me one good thing you did at tryouts." And he would find one. After a few more days of this, he began to text me, "Mom, today my small victory was . . ."

Once, in the classroom I had been consulting a student who was distraught over a low test grade, and the student's dialogue was, "I didn't know anything. I'm too dumb for this class." Without even thinking about it, I responded, "Let's find a small victory here. Let's talk about all the problems you got right; those are things you do know." Afterwards, the student was not as upset as he was when we started, and I'd like to think that he felt better about himself.

Celebrate small victories. Powerful words that will reshape your attitude, your outlook, and your interactions with others. That's what those three words have done for me.

23

Believe in the Goodwill of Your Instructor

[Luke] I can't believe it.
[Yoda] That is why you fail.

— Star Wars Episode V:
The Empire Strikes Back (1980)

S ome women won't roll with certain people. They will only roll with other women, or small people, or the coach. I was explaining this curiosity to someone after telling them a story about a practice where I was partnered with a burly guy I didn't know. We were learning a choke from the back that day. Coach showed the move, and then we went to our area to drill. Drill is when you practice the new move back and forth between partners. I'm well aware of the idea of practicing at "game speed," but in my experience at the gym, drill was conducted at moderate speed. My partner apparently thought drill was sparring because he was choking me hard. I got lightheaded and saw stars—that's how tight his choke was. I'm thinking that Coach will say something as he's walking around because surely he sees that my partner thinks he's rolling for a medal. But, no, nothing was said. I told myself, *I just have to get through drill, then I'll never roll with this guy again.*

Not to be . . . because on this day, instead of letting us pick our partners for sparring, Coach assigned partners. And who does he choose as my partner?—same guy. The look on my face must have read "you've got to be kidding," because Coach said, "Oh, so you've already decided you can't do it?" *Humph, I can do it, but I might not live, but fine—be that way.* Now there was no way I was not going to roll with this guy: *I'll show you.* In Coaching 101, we call this mind-fucking. I dove in and rolled. And the guy rolled hard. Knee-on-belly times ten, heavy transitions, mount to armbars and chokes.

As I told this story to my friend, she was shocked: "What a jerk. Why didn't you say you wouldn't do it? You have to protect yourself. I mean, that's one of your rights."

"Yeah, yeah, I suppose."

And then she more thoughtfully asked, "What do you think of those women who won't roll with guys like that?"

Without hesitating, I said, "That they are pussies."

That night after class, however, I wasn't thinking about anyone else's rolling preferences. I was pissed. I mean I was really stewing.

"Damn freaking beast probably hates women. What the hell, I can't believe I had to roll with him—that Coach made me roll with him when he knows that guy is an a-hole." (Actually, he is a nice guy, but this was my first impression.) I harbored ill will that night at class. I wouldn't even look at Coach after that. I felt like I had been someone's grappling dummy. After class, I grabbed my stuff and stormed outside to my car. Naturally I had a text from coach Brick asking, "How was class?"

I just started bawling. All I could do was talk to myself:

What are you doing?

No one takes you seriously.

Why do you do this?

You are just in there getting beat up on.

And then I took some deep breaths and regained my composure. It's interesting how lucid you can be when Gollum stops arguing with Sméagol in your head. I was struck by a single thought: *James is your coach.* And Saulo Ribeiro says, "Believe in the goodwill of your instructor."

At that very moment, it all became very clear. I knew that Coach would not put me into a situation he didn't think I could handle. I knew he had my best interest in mind. And if it was a test, then I had passed.

I hadn't quit. I didn't lie there and do nothing during the sparring session. No, I battled. In fact, I think The Guy only submitted me once. Or maybe he didn't submit me at all . . . I don't recall . . . because the entire roll was a whirlwind of survival and rebellion against the injustice of it all. Still, I stuck it out.

I learned some great lessons that night. Achievement involves taking risks. Coach had called my bluff. It requires effort and challenge to be your best. Discipline is doing what is hard and necessary. What I was doing was work, hard work. Other people believed in me, so I had to believe in myself. Once I could overcome what was holding me back—or just admit to and honor it—then I could know what I needed to do to move forward.

It's hard to put ourselves into situations that will challenge our chutzpah. We fear not being good enough. That's why we have to give ourselves over to trust. We have to believe that we have surrounded ourselves with quality people who care about us and who will help us stay the course toward whatever our measure of personal achievement might be.

24

Leave Your Ego in the Gym Bag

Welcome to Foster's Chop Shop—
We Dismantle Egos

T he ego is a terrible taskmaster. It taunts some people into a muscle tee and swagger, and suggests they enter a gym that advertises MMA on its sign. Foster's is primarily a Jiu-Jitsu gym, but it does offer some classes in MMA. Jiu-Jitsu has become an essential part of the mixed martial artist's skill set, so people, mostly men, come to the gym thinking they will be the next great cage fighter. Some enter the gym thinking they are already the next great cage fighter. You can always tell who these guys are. They walk into the gym like everyone has been waiting for them to show up. Their chests are either puffed out or maybe slouched over (because the weight of their massive pecs makes it hard to stand up straight). They sign the waiver to participate with nonchalance as if they are telling themselves, "I hope everyone else signed one of these because I am gonna do some pun-ish-ing to-day!" After they whip off their oversized hoodie, they step into the gym in their flashy fight shorts and skull-covered rash guard. Coach has an innate sense of these guys. He will look at them the way you look at a person who has bad BO, but is the only person who doesn't know it.

With the restraint of a saint, Coach will give them the skinny on gym protocol and talk to them about lining up when class gets ready to start. Newbies are at the end of the line. These cocky guys always seem insulted that their superior talents are not recognized and they must stand to the left of the lowliest white belts. Usually their eyes are shifting around, and they bounce on their toes trying to seem calm and collected, but we see them flex their biceps and touch their abs as if trying to draw our attention to their impressiveness. If you talk to them, they will usually tell you about their extensive fighting history and the number of hours of TiVo'd UFC they have watched.

Most, but not all, get gassed out during warmup. Of course to them, warmup is a waste of time because they came here to "punish some peo-ple." And unlike the humble rest of us, who recognize that our Jiu-Jitsu needs improvement and who are eager to learn new moves, these guys already know everything, so they won't ask for help. In fact, many will try to tell you what to do because—of course—they already know it all. Maybe it *is* possible to learn everything from YouTube.

When it comes time to spar, Coach will not usually let new guys roll. Instead, they must watch or keep time. This is out of respect for their safety. But Coach has a sixth sense for these cocky guys. They tell him they have years of experience already and are raring to go. I love this part. So Coach will relent, as if impressed, and have these guys roll with the upper belts for a while. During these rounds, the cocky guys are trying to muscle their way through their opponents with no technique at all. They are jumping, tumbling, grabbing, and scrambling all out of control. The buzzer goes off, and they pop up: "Hey, no problem. Kicked his ass." Eyes are going back and forth checking to see who saw them.

All the while, Coach is watching from another ring, biding his time like a cougar stalking his prey. Not as easy as it looks on television, huh? And then he invites them to roll with him. They stand up a little straighter, try to hide that they have been gasping for breath, and act as if: "Finally, someone of my caliber."

They recapture their swagger, shake hands, and "it's time to punish some peo-ple"—only it's them who gets punished. Hungry for some humble pie? It's like a submission seminar. Coach takes no prisoners. He often seems to channel Ironman, like he's murmuring, "Do you recognize my authority now?"

First it's an armbar, then a choke from the top, the back, the side. Coach will toss them left, right, over, under, and put them in triangles and guillotines. They try to be tough at first and not tap, so Coach puts the squeeze on nice and slow, like he's deflating the ego in their fat heads and giving them a chance to save some face. It has been said that egotism is the anesthetic that dulls the pain of stupidity. Well, stupidity should hurt. Some of these guys save nothing and can barely make it to the end of the line to bow out. A few will figure it out and admit that maybe, even though they once won a bar brawl, they are not the next Anderson Silva (the current UFC Middleweight Champion and the promotion's longest reigning champion). You might see those guys again, but the deflated ones never return, which is really no loss. They leave and then tell their friends what a crappy gym it is—full of pussies. We know better. Our gym is full of confident, quality people. So what if we humiliate a prick every now and then.

25

Go with the Flow

The colloquialism "go with the flow" is used as a training mantra inside many Jiu-Jitsu gyms. It may seem, on the surface, that this is a simple directive to move seamlessly and in concert with your opponent. As a student new to Jiu-Jitsu, I found out that "go" and "flow" have many meanings and that the only seamless movement I could make occurred while I was standing in lineup. I also found that uncovering the secrets of "going with the flow" was helpful in navigating my journey through grief.

The "flow drill" is often assigned to us as a warm up exercise. In the flow drill, you roll in a non-combative manner with your partner and allow things to just happen. If you are in position to get swept, you let the sweep transpire and then flow into your defensive position. Your instinct wants to fight the sweep, shift your weight, and protectively reposition your body. You eventually learn to just go with the moment by calming your conscious mind. If your partner is reinforcing the learning experience, they willingly accept your new position and let you maneuver into the next offense. In this relaxed situation, you are able to feel the subtle dynamics that are taking place without anxiety making you tense and resistant.

The legendary Jiu-Jitsu master Rickson Gracie is credited with saying, "Flow with the go." This perspective puts more emphasis on the "go," or what is happening to you. As a life lesson, I see that mantra as a constructive way to accept what is happening to us and to develop countermeasures that are safe for us physically and mentally.

We all have a way of letting our habits gain momentum. Our habits can carry us into a mindless and unfeeling state from one comfortable, or uncomfortable, situation into the next. Like muscle memory, our habits can help us flow. But our habits can also hinder us. Our physical and mental habits can keep us from moving forward and growing as athletes and as human beings.

Coach helps us identify our habits with a training drill called "Chess." Very much like the board game chess, this drill takes place one move at a time with your partner. You start in an agreed-upon position—for example, closed guard. Whoever is going first (usually the person with the higher rank) makes only one move. One move means grabbing their left sleeve with your right hand, putting one foot on the mat, or shifting your right hip to the left. One move does not mean executing a technique in its entirety.

This drill accomplishes many things. It forces you to plan several steps ahead. It forces you to counter your opponent's move while formulating your own attack. And your opponent is, likewise, planning to counter your move. You can only be successful at this drill by consciously and skillfully executing the "go" and not falling into the traps of your habitual moves. I have trouble with this drill because I am not yet skillful enough to plan many steps in advance. I also have trouble because I become more focused on what I am planning than on what is happening at present. And I have many habits that do not always advance my position. This drill gives me anxiety. There is too much time to worry that I have made, or am going to make, the wrong move. And there are no take-backs.

My expenditure of emotional energy on things I have done wrong is much greater than the energy I use to recognize things I have done right. The isolation of moves in the chess drill provides an opportunity to practice being more compassionate to myself. If you were observing this drill, you would likely see two types of people. There are the people who make a move and radiate confidence. These are the people who have already embarked on a path to victory in their own minds. And there is the other group—the group that moves a foot and immediately sighs or rolls their eyes or says, "dang it," because they already believe that they have embarked on a futile path. Like a physical habit and its muscle memory, this behavior reinforces negative mental habits or neural memory. Negative habits include thoughts of self-depreciation that lead us to give up on ourselves. These are the negative habits that keep us fighting discomfort and uncertainty instead of learning to live with those feelings and discover who we can fully be.

There is a great deal of physical discomfort in Jiu-Jitsu. It's obvious to most people that having an arm hyperextended, a shoulder locked, or a neck squeezed between the back of someone's shin and thigh can cause discomfort. What might not be so obvious is the mental discomfort. When I first started training, I would tap at the slightest sensation of physical discomfort, and I would tap if I believed I was going to experience a slight sensation of discomfort. I would panic if my arms got pinned in positions that made me feel vulnerable, although it didn't hurt. I would also panic in certain positions that made me feel claustrophobic.

Much of the mental discomfort I experienced from grief felt a lot like the mental discomfort of Jiu-Jitsu. Nervous, anxious, claustrophobic, insecure, vulnerable. I was a beginning griever just like I was a beginner BJJ practitioner. I had to practice being in uncomfortable positions. Just like it is easier to tap than to battle, it was easier to avoid dealing with thoughts that made me sad and turn to unproductive behaviors. Combating discomfort in Jiu-Jitsu is dealt with head-on. If you hate being trapped in side control, then Coach has you start each sparring session trapped in side control. If we are learning an escape, Coach has us practice it from "worst case scenario" position. This usually means that your opponent has control of your head and a dominant starting point. When I was training to compete and was uncomfortable scrambling to position, I had to start all my sessions lying on my belly instead of starting on my knees, forcing me to quickly scramble to an advantageous position.

Over time I found that I could stay in an uncomfortable situation longer and longer and not panic. With practice, I learned to not be so afraid and to relax into the position and defend myself thoughtfully. I started small. Sometimes I would tell myself to take one more breath before I tapped, that I had to hang in there for a moment longer than my initial submission response told me to. It took time, and it took practice. It took not avoiding positions I didn't like, but instead using them as opportunities to put more tools in my toolbox and more courage in my heart.

I was training armbars with Brick one practice, and Brick was praising the strength and consistency of my armbar. My response to him was, "Now all I have to do is get on the top, and I'll be fine." Coach, who was nearby and has satellite-dish ears, (figuratively, not literally) heard what I said and, as astutely as ever, remarked, "You need to think that you will be fine from any position." *Ah, yes. Right again.* As long as I kept thinking that I would be more successful in one position than another, I would continue to hold myself back.

I was holding myself back in the grieving process as well. I wanted to protect myself against discomfort. I didn't want to "go with the flow." I didn't want to go to the places that made my heart break over and over again. Seems like a logical survival instinct to protect ourselves from discomfort, doesn't it? Cold? Put on a coat. Hungry? Get something to eat. However, protecting myself from my emotional discomfort was not helping me survive it.

In the gym, we could recreate a worst-case scenario. But I would never want to recreate my emotional worst-case scenario. Lisa and Kathleen both encouraged me to be honest about these feelings to myself. During my personal "quiet time," when my mind was supposed to be free from worry, I was to allow myself to think about those deep feelings that I feared . . . but only for a short period of time. (I bought three sand timers with durations of one, two, and three minutes.) During that short period, I was to feel those deep emotions as fully as I could let myself. I had to live in those feelings and acknowledge them. I had to honor that they were a new and acceptable part of who I was. Through this process, I learned that to feel with such intensity, which left me drained and aching, is a feature of being human. I learned this was a gift—to be able to go there, visit those intense thoughts, and then let them be. I thought I was broken, that I had to fix these thoughts to be whole again. But I didn't. I had to let them be my "go," and I had to let them teach me a healthy way to flow within the world again.

26

Echo of Unanswered Questions

One day, Kathleen shared with me that people often ask her how she can do the work that she does, counseling people through grief and life transitions. She said that her work has shown her that there are basically three groups of people: those who never recover and digress to a state of abandoned reality; those who move forward in an emotionless state as if their tragedy never happened, alienating all compassion; and those who rejoin life, finding a new way to define themselves not as their tragedy, but as people who have suffered and endured to live again. It is the latter group that gives her hope and encourages her to continue the work she does.

After telling me this, she smiled and said that she saw me in the last group—the group that found a way to survive and be happy again. Is it ironic that I started crying? I did not feel like a success story. I was consumed with turbulent ideas: *I'm not done yet. I haven't figured it all out yet. I'm still scared.*

Am I scared because I still can't get my heart and my head around why I feel this was done to me? Is it because death tortures those who are left behind, not those who have left us? Do all grieving parents ask what they did wrong for something this horrifying to happen? Do all grieving parents question every mistake they ever made, every injustice they may have placed upon another person?

We don't want sympathy, and we don't want empathy. To accept sympathy is victimizing. To accept empathy suggests others have suffered what we have suffered, and I personally have a hard time accepting that kind of pain in another person. Perhaps that is why grieving people are so hard to support emotionally, especially in the acute phase of grief. For us to accept empathy brings forth guilt that others have suffered. We are also angry at the suggestion that anyone could possibly have suffered as terribly as we have. And even if someone's story is equally traumatic, our story is ours alone—we are walking in the only moccasins that we give a rip about. It's a vicious mind game where the rules keep changing—we can't cheat and we can't win. And we can't be the ref or on the sidelines—we have to play. And no matter who we are, we can never be prepared to participate in that kind of contest.

The death of a child is the worst imaginable experience a parent can face. Not only do we torture ourselves with the sinful vanity of our pasts, we become consumed with an anger that can easily destroy us. Even when our rational brain tells us there was nothing we could have done to prevent what happened, our irrational brain is full of the acrimonious commentary: if only . . . what if . . . .why didn't I . . . ?

I can picture that night in the hotel room vividly, like it was yesterday. The scene wreaks havoc on any compassion I may offer myself. Did I call 911 fast enough? Did I do CPR right? Should I have pushed harder? Was it something I let her eat? To be completely honest, I admit to a bruise on my heart, a place where I can't forgive myself. A painful bruise of responsibility. A feeling that if I had saved her, then so many people would not have to be sad, would not have to miss their sister, their friend, their teammate. A feeling that when people look at me, I remind them that she is gone.

A mother's heart says we protect our babies at all costs. I tried, but I couldn't save Carly. I was the only one there in the room, so I am the only one to know what it was like. I was the one who had to call her father and her grandparents. And yet, what if I hadn't been there? What if I had decided not to go on that trip? That would have been an even worse guilt. I could never recover. I am eternally grateful that the person who was there with Carly was me and not someone else—me, who loved her more than I loved myself.

It's said that people grieve as hard as they love. To be sure, every one of my trillion cells was proving that, aching with unbearable pain.

As I grieved, I was also tormented with wanting to direct my anger at something or someone. I certainly couldn't direct my anger at Carly. The torment of this conundrum is unbearable at times. In cases where a child is in a car accident, the parent might say, "Why did I let them drive?" Or the parent might direct anger at others involved in the accident. Or let's say a child is dying of a known illness; the parent can be mad at the illness, the doctors, the lack of a cure.

But what about me? Where do I direct my anger? I have no closure because I have no diagnosis. My beautiful, healthy, athletic daughter was completely asymptomatic and then she died—a girl who could run up and down a basketball court for hours, who could solo on a saxophone in an auditorium full of people, who was seldom sick and perpetually full of verve and an enviable passion for life. How does her heart just go crazy in the blink of an eye?

After Carly's death, we put my boys through a full cardiac workup at Children's Hospital. The pediatric cardiologist suggested that Carly had long QT syndrome, but did not see any signs of it in the boys. We learned that this condition is more prevalent in males, but more fatal in females. We learned that there are three variations of long QT. Two of the variants cause "episodes" from which the person can usually be revived. The mildest form causes people to faint often. The moderate form can cause fainting or cause the heart to stop briefly or beat irregularly. The third form is the one where the person has had no episodes—the first symptom is death.

The doctor inferred long QT as the culprit because Carly did not have hypercardiomyopathy, a blood clot, or any microbiological or toxicological evidence to support otherwise.

But that was not good enough for me. We pursued a genetic test, because there are several gene markers that have recently been discovered for long QT. This fairly new genetic test has a twenty-five- to thirty-percent chance of false negative and is still under development (science is uncovering new gene markers almost daily), but I still wanted it done. There is only one laboratory in the United States that does the test, which costs $5,000 and involves mapping of the entire genome. The logistics failed us. Carly's tissue samples were in a North Carolina laboratory, which apparently did not store the samples at the temperature required for successful genetics testing. The genetics laboratory reported that they had tried, but were unsuccessful in getting what they needed from the samples. I knew enough about molecular biology and biotechnology to ask, "How can that be?" It is possible to get DNA from a drop of blood. Science has polymerase chain reaction machines to amplify samples. How can the genetics laboratory not have enough information from Carly's tissue samples? I felt that the discipline to which I had dedicated much of my adult life had let me down—and hard.

I still have no answers. That I may never know haunts me. Some people ask why it haunts me. They say that finding out won't bring her back. I'm painfully aware of that fact. But to have some answers, then I will have somewhere to direct my anger or perhaps more easily embrace some degree of acceptance.

"A lot of things haven't been answered in our life— and we are still searching for the questions."

— Chögyam Trungpa

27

Butterflies

When Carly was in kindergarten, she wrote a little piece of piano music with lyrics as an entry for the school district's Reflections contest. The Reflections contest is sponsored by the national parent-teacher-student association to bring notice to student work in the fine arts: music, drawing, painting, and photography. Each year, the contest has a theme and the submitted works must reflect the theme as interpreted by the artist. That year the theme was "Wouldn't it be great . . ." Carly's piece of music was titled, "Wouldn't it be Great if I was a Caterpillar?" The music exceeded my nonexistent musical ability, but was certainly age-appropriate and skillful for a kindergartener. I loved the lyrics. It told the story of a little caterpillar on a leaf; the caterpillar eats the leaf and goes into a cocoon, and the lyrics end with, "Wouldn't it be great if I was a caterpillar because then I could turn into a butterfly." The lyrics describe coming out of the cocoon with beautiful, colorful wings and flying away.

My memory of this song is reinforced by a story my mom likes to tell. While visiting friends at holiday time in the San Francisco Bay area, my mom, like any proud grandparent, asked Carly to "do" her "Caterpillar Song." Carly agreed, then became perplexed when she realized my mother's friend did not have a piano. "That's okay," she chirped, "I'll do a dance with it." And off she went singing her song and doing an interpretive dance. She got down in a little ball when the caterpillar was in the cocoon and then rose up as the butterfly was emerging. What I wouldn't give for a video of that performance. Carly was so spontaneously creative.

And so butterflies have always been associated with Carly. She would sit, still and patient, in the butterfly museum of the local zoo and wait for as long as it took for at least one to land on her.

The longer we are on this Earth, the more time there is for extraordinary pieces of our life to entwine themselves and bring to light an even greater significance than any event has on its own.

During one of my sessions with Kathleen, she shared an insight she had while attending a presentation given by a lepidopterist (a butterfly expert). The expert was describing how butterflies develop when Kathleen was struck by a revelation that butterfly development paralleled the experiences of her grieving clients.

When a caterpillar is wrapped up inside its cocoon, it becomes a gooey mess. Nothing is added to the gooey mess during this stage and nothing is taken away—it is a protected mess of churning protoplasm.

This is how people who are grieving feel. Our insides are a churning mess of emotional soup: chunks of anger, slices of pain, a dash or two of guilt, pinch of doubt, all agitating in a thick broth of sadness. So we cocoon ourselves. We close up with avoidance tactics. We wrap ourselves tightly in our own arms because we are the only arms that can do the job that needs to be done . . . the waiting job. During this stage, no one can help us. No one can give us anything. We are closed off.

Growth is all about timing. As the protoplasm churns, it begins to piece itself together into essential butterfly parts. The reassembly cannot be rushed. The butterfly cannot come out too soon. And the butterfly must get itself out of that cocoon as well. There is no assistance from other butterflies.

Moving through the grieving process is also about timing. Each person, like each species of butterfly, has a reassembly pace that only they endure. As much as the people outside of our cocoon would like to hurry us through reassembly, we cannot. To rush the healing process risks placing gaps in our stability. And likewise, no one can assist us during our own reassembly. It is for us to do alone.

The effort taken by a butterfly to exit its cocoon is part of the developmental process. The effort is exercise, which squeezes vital fluids to their organs and aids the elimination of lingering wastes. The protoplasm looks like a butterfly now. It emerges and rests. It is not ready yet to fly away. Given some time to dry off and move the last of the internal fluids through its new delicate and colorful wings, the butterfly will eventually launch and begin its new life. The caterpillar has been transformed.

With time and protection, grieving people also exit their cocoons. We come out only when we are ready. We come out whole, but new.

28

Succeed Not Cede

Sometimes when you feel like giving up, you have to remind yourself why you held on for so long in the first place. I remember a training session where I had really wanted to give up. Jeff B ran the competition team class, and we'd had an especially tough workout that day.

Of note, Jeff's workouts are approached by prudent team members with respectful trepidation. Most sessions end with, "For all of you who puked, thank you. Way to go hard."

Jeff is about five foot four and "a buck thirty-five," but his presence looms about the gym as if he were Kratos, the winged enforcer of Zeus and god of strength, might, and power. He is in perpetual motion, buoyed by four pots of coffee and four hours of sleep a day. He has trouble getting his body fat above two percent. Jeff has a brown belt in Jiu-Jitsu, and in addition to his own fight training, he coaches fighters; directs, promotes, and officiates the local BJJ tournament The Revolution; officiates for the International Brazilian Jiu-Jitsu Federation; and has a "regular" job, a beautiful wife, and a couple of kids. Jeff was a featured fighter in the independent film Walking to the Cage (directed by Matt Hickney) and sports the cage name "Corporal Punishment." Just in case you might fear Jeff, let his image be properly balanced by the fact that Jeff has strutted to the cage to the beat of the Sesame Street theme song. Lastly, Jeff has tattoos on the top of his feet. On one is the kanji symbol for honor, and on the other, the symbol for courage. Jeff is, quite literally, a man who walks his talk.

I must have stayed for the next class after competition team, because somehow on this particular day, I was rolling with a gal who had never done the competition class. She was big and strong and a good opponent for me. Class was nearly over, and I was basically riding out the clock, to be completely honest. She had gotten me in side control (or maybe it was a mount) and was holding me down pretty well. I was exhausted. I had that tight-throat feeling and didn't want to struggle anymore. Coach and Jeff were on the periphery, and I remember saying, "I'm done," hoping it was just loud enough to have her hear me, but not so loud that Coach could hear me. I'd wanted to tap because I wanted to stop, not because she had submitted me. And then I heard Coach say, "You can stop when you get out. You have to escape."

No! Why? My spirit was in conflict. I don't consider myself a quitter, but I felt beaten, and at that moment, I was willing to relinquish my pride and quit. It felt disgraceful to think that way: part of me thinking *what does it matter if I stop?* and part of me feeling like I shouldn't stop. It's hard to do in-depth soul-searching, however, when you are in the midst of a Jiu-Jitsu sparring session.

The next thing I knew, Jeff was on his belly right by my head so I could see him, and he was calmly giving me instructions. I tried to execute the moves he was telling me to do, but maybe because part of me still wanted to give up or maybe because she was doing a good job, or both, I wasn't very successful. This just frustrated me more.

"I want to stop. I'm done." Those statements were not acknowledged. Jeff just kept telling me to breathe and where to put my hands and feet. That he was so calm and clear was an indication that I could do it; I just had to keep doing the work. And I got out eventually. It is hard to describe the feeling you get when you escape from under a tough opponent. "Relief" just doesn't cover it.

In the other sports I'd played, I always had a ball or a net between me and my opponents. I always had teammates who could pick up the slack if I was having an off day. In Jiu-Jitsu, the only person who can save you is you. Jiu-Jitsu truly calls you out, challenges you: "Let's see what you got. What are you really made of?"

And this is analogous to experiencing a life trauma. That's when nature calls you out. Anyone can give up—that's definitely the easiest thing to do. I wanted to give up many times after Carly died because healing was too hard. Instead, sleeping, drinking, isolating myself, running away—these behaviors taunted me to just let it all go, give up. But something inside me made me hang on. Some primitive survival instinct helped me chip through that wall of self-doubt. I don't recall ever being conscious of it. That instinct, coupled with the external support of a few key people, kept me from going over the edge. I felt encouraged to make a better effort.

After that spar, I apologized to Jeff. I felt sorry that I hadn't been tougher, that I had wanted to stop. He just shook his head, reminding me that those thoughts were not important. That I didn't stop was what was important. I suppose he's been on that precipice before: the one-on-one combat where giving up can mean injury or death. As an athlete and a coach, like many of the people in the gym, he is incredibly mentally tough. During workout, he is always intensely vocal about how your mind has to take over when your body wants to stop. Sometimes your greatest asset is your ability to stay with something longer than anyone else.

I learned a lot during that practice session. I took many thoughts home with me:

(1) It does not feel good to be trapped on the bottom, so don't get yourself there.

(2) If you do get there, relax and remind yourself that you know what to do.

(3) Listen to the support units around you.

(4) Don't listen to the quitter in your head.

(5) No one else expects you to fall apart, so why should you?

(6) Remember that the feeling you get when you give the second/third/fourth effort is infinitely more rewarding than the feeling of just "being done."

29

O Ye of Little Faith

We are never trapped in life, and yet it can feel that way. I think one of the side effects of Carly's death, which is painful for my parents, is that now I question my faith. Does that mean I didn't have enough to start with? What I know is that right now I am not comforted by my faith. I went back to church for a while afterwards because my parents thought I should. They are so rock solid in this arena, it is enviable to me. But I can't get to that place, and I feel like I am disappointing them. I didn't get much out of sitting in the back of church by myself, hoping no one would talk to me, or from crying the moment I walked in. I used to leave before Mass was over because I would either run out of tissue or hyperventilate out of fear. I had so much anger at God. Did You take her? Why would You do that? Why did You take a girl who loved the life You gave her? A girl who honored her existence with passion and energy and good will, who loved her parents, her brothers, and her friends.

Every day I work with kids who are throwing their lives away making bad choices. I see parents who ignore and belittle their children. I see crime and violence in the news every day. Those people are alive. Why not them instead of Carly?

My anger at God lessened somewhat when it was obvious that it wasn't getting me anywhere or giving me any answers. So I tried a new approach. I began to believe that death is random. We have no control over it; it can happen at any moment. Scary! And let's just say that God is there waiting for us, ready to comfort us because He has no control over death either—it's part of the life cycle of which we are all a part. This approach didn't make me feel much better either. Instead, it sort of heightened my anxiety. However, it did bring to light the fragility of life and reinforce the need for daily kindnesses.

Lisa once asked me if my outlook on death has changed, and I emphatically responded with a yes. Five years ago, I seldom thought of death and certainly not in the realm of my immediate family. Sure, I worried about Chuck driving home late at night from gigs, but I felt strongly at the time that if something happened to Chuck, I would get through. I would have to be strong for my kids. Never ever had the idea of one of my children dying been given serious thought.

After Carly died, I didn't care if I died. Actually—more accurately—I didn't want to die, but I didn't care if I lived. Sometimes I just wanted to sleep forever. And I would—and still do—tell myself that it would be okay to die because then I will see Carly again. Actually it's more of a concession: I want to live for my boys, but should something happen, the people I leave behind should know that I'm with Carly and that's okay.

Where am I with faith now? Pretty stuck. I do believe that I will see Carly again, that she is happy and in a good place doing good work. I bet she is the best darn guardian angel in the regiment. When Carly had decided what instrument she wanted to play in jazz band, she announced, "I want to play alto sax because it's the main instrument in the band—right in the middle with most of the solos." Yeah, not a shy kid, definitely liked to be front and center. I'm sure she has all the other angels on a schedule and working to be the best they can be. There is probably a competitive bracket set up keeping track of who touches the most lives. And if God is there, she's probably checking to make sure He can shoot a left-handed layup.

> *"People often think about trying to hold back their tears, but as human beings, we should take pride in our capacity to be sad and happy."*
>
> — Chogyam Trungpa
> *Overcoming Physical Materialism*

30

My Secret Life

I 've already mentioned that people grieve differently. Chuck and I were also warned that grief can destroy a marriage. And indeed it can really test a relationship. Chuck has always supported my "whimsies" as he calls them. Like when I go crazy, painting the walls of the house different colors or changing the downstairs bathroom to a jungle theme. I have always immersed myself in different projects, and Chuck knows that when I decide to do something, I go all out . . . reading books about the subject, buying all the supplies I need, taking over the dining room table, or taking over the garage and using the ping-pong table as my workbench. Chuck is really laid back—a lovely Libra. He just wants me to be happy, and I love that about him. So it's no surprise to me that he stays out of my Jiu-Jitsu. I like that too—it's my thing. I have tried to show him a couple of moves, but he won't have any of that. He reminds me that when I was taking striking class, I had goaded him into punching the bag (his recollection not mine) and that he hurt his wrist and it ached for several weeks. It would probably kill him if I demonstrated the rear naked choke.

Chuck had this exchange with our good friend Jenny. (Jenny told me about it.)

[Chuck] "My wife has a secret life. She leaves the house three or four times a week at night, and I don't know where she goes or who she is with."

[Jenny laughing] "Yes you do. She goes to Jiu-Jitsu."

[Chuck] "No, she goes to (air quotes) 'roll.'"

———

Chuck had this exchange with my parents when they were out together, and I was training.

[Chuck] "I don't think Elena is ever going to like golf."

Enough said there.

———

Chuck had this exchange with me on a rare night we went out together; it was our anniversary, two weeks after Worlds.

[Chuck] "Are those new jeans?"

[Me] "No, I've had them, but you haven't seen them because they haven't fit for a while."

[Chuck] "Hm."

[Me] "But I might need some new jeans if I go down a weight class for my next competition."

[Chuck] "You know, most women want to lose weight to wear a slinky dress. You want to lose weight so you can go beat people up."

———

It was Christmas, and I had been training at Jiu-Jitsu for a little over a year. One of my gifts from Chuck was a Jiu-Jitsu skills book with this inscription: "E, after seeing the pictures in Chapter 4, I have decided to hire a private detective. C"

The title of that chapter: "The Mount."

———

It was Chuck's birthday, and we were meeting some of his friends at a bar to celebrate. I arrived late because I'd been training. So I rushed into the bar to get my party on, and someone asked, "How was your practice?"

I impulsively replied, "Great! I had the best roll with Owen."

Silence. Eyes shifted to Chuck. "You okay with this?"

Chuck just shrugged. "Happens all the time."

31

Hello Worlds

I gave up coaching. I committed to improving my breathing. I continued to work toward emotional stability. But to what end? In the back of my head, I had wanted to train for Pan Ams that March, but the whole ordeal with the doctor saying I should have surgery had crushed my confidence, and I didn't feel ready. But something kept nagging me like a tiny sliver—you can't see it, but it keeps poking you. The next big tournament was the World Championships in June. It's a huge tournament in southern California. That would give me five months to train. I felt that if I committed to it, I could be ready to compete in June. I knew that if I made my intentions public, I would follow through. I needed something bigger than just me to hold myself accountable to my goal.

I don't have a history of letting a lot of people know what I am doing. Maybe it's because I wonder why anyone would care. Maybe it's because I think it's none of their business. Maybe it's because if I don't follow through, then I won't be letting people down. I let myself down all the time, but I never let other people down. When my friend was training for her first marathon, she asked me to train with her. The deal was that when she called I would meet her, rain or shine, whatever hour, and I always did. She needed me to make herself train, she said. Years later, I decided to run a marathon, but I didn't tell anyone—except my immediate family because I had to be gone for several hours at a time. After it was over and word got out, my friend asked me why I didn't ask her to train with me. I assured her it wasn't personal, that I hadn't asked anyone to train with me. I knew I would run the marathon no matter what—I had promised my sister-in-law that I would, it was her idea (she's an ultra-marathoner)—but what if I didn't want to follow a training plan, if I ran slowly, or if I wanted to stop in the middle? Who really cared if I was training to run a marathon anyway? But I couldn't train for a Jiu-Jitsu tournament by myself. I needed help, lots of help.

First, I had to ask Coach if he would support me in going to Worlds. Before a tournament of any size, Coach will announce that anyone interested in competing should talk to him, and attend the competition-team classes, and ramp up the number of training days. Well, I had already been working out with the competition team for over a year because I liked the challenging workouts, and I was already training three days a week. But I had never asked to compete in a tournament. There were times when I had competed locally, and those were times when Brick basically told me that I was going to do it, so I did. It hadn't been an intentional and personal decision on my part.

I put off asking Coach for a couple of practices, telling myself it was bad timing, Coach was busy . . . whatever I could do to stall. I knew I was being childish, but I felt like I was a little kid asking for permission to borrow the car when I didn't have my license.

When I finally asked Coach after a practice, my knee caps were shaking and I had to force myself to make direct eye contact: *If you don't look confident, he's never going to say yes.* There were parts of me that didn't think he would say yes, and I would be crushed, and there were parts of me that hoped he wouldn't say yes, and I would be relieved. Conflicted? You bet. I realized quickly that I would be more crushed than relieved when he didn't answer me right away. It was a pause of a couple of seconds, but it was plenty long enough for me to mentally recite a litany of reasons why I shouldn't go and how could I have possibly thought I deserved to travel with a team of people that I held in such high esteem. And then he said, "Sure. I'll support you in that." Gulp.

I'm pretty sure my knee caps were still quivering when I got home, and my stomach was all a jumble at the decision I had just made, but I walked into the living room, where everyone was watching television, and announced, "Tonight I made a commitment to be in a big tournament in June, and I'm going to be training really hard, and I'm going to need your support because this is something I really want to do." The heads all nodded as if I'd just announced I wanted to repaint the kitchen. Still, it was important to make this public so I could not back out.

> *"I will stand and fight. You know I will. But I need a little help here."*
>
> — Jake Sully, *Avatar,* 2009

One thing I can be counted on to do is follow through. I may be mediocre, but I am diligent. I may be late, but I will always show up. I may struggle, but I will always work hard. In the end, I knew this tournament would be about my integrity and the quality of my preparation. What I didn't know was that the lessons I would learn on this five-month journey-within-a-journey would change my life.

Five months was going to pass by fast. They would span the spring months that were always difficult for me. Would my commitment give me the focus to see myself through that time period without self-destructing? I knew I needed to get off to a strong start. I knew that I would have to commit to those final nutritional changes I was being stubborn about. At Lisa's bidding, I did cut back on my coffee. It wasn't so much a matter of caffeine as it was a hindrance to my digestion. The acidity of the coffee and the stress I was swallowing daily were keeping me from absorbing all the nutrients I needed. I was already eating pretty well, but I wasn't maximizing the nutrients my food had to offer. So, yes, I gave up coffee. And yes, I gave up drinking. For five months, I did not drink any alcohol. Previously I had not gone five days without drinking. When we were invited out to dinner, I would tell our hosts before I got there that I was in training and not drinking. That was so much easier than showing up and having to deal with that glass in front of me and the looks of astonishment. During that spring, our Foundation fundraiser was a wine tasting, and I did not imbibe even at that event. I didn't eat white flour or refined sugar. I had detoxified my body. For the first time, I was eating because food was my fuel, not my antidepressant.

And I worked hard in the gym. I went to class four or more days a week and often did two or three classes a day. In April, I added hills and sprints to improve my endurance. That is when Lisa made me drink the beet juice.

"Where's the literature to support this insult to my palate?" I had asked her.

Yes, there was a study done where they gave Olympic athletes two ounces of fresh beet juice before training, and they had improved stamina. Beet juice increases the oxygen-carrying capacity of the red blood cells. It is also high in antioxidants, can lower blood pressure, and cleanses the blood. Too bad it tastes like dirt even after you peel the beets. Honestly, I tried cutting it with fruit juice, soy milk, and adding ginger, but in the end I just went for the good old college "throw back." Bypass the taste buds and down the hatch. I had made a commitment to be my best come June. My Jiu-Jitsu skills would have to stand on their own, but I knew I had control over the way I prepared my body. I did not want a lack of conditioning to contribute in any way to poor performance.

In a previous chapter, I mention the harness, which was introduced to me by Brick. The harness is a vest that straps you to rubber tubing, which your teammate holds to provide resistance as you run the length of the gym down and back for a prescribed period of time. My first harness session lasted for two minutes. Dang. Apparently the extra conditioning I was doing was not enough, because the harness was torture. My quads were burning, and my throat was squeezing up. I felt like I was coughing up alveoli for hours after I was done.

It sucked, but over time the harness became a measure of my cardio improvement. A week before Worlds, I was doing three or four sessions of three-minute rounds, and I would jog or swing kettle bells in between sessions. It was awesome. I felt great. I was able to smile even though it was always hard. And I felt an immeasurable sense of accomplishment when I was finished. For the last four long years, I felt that I couldn't finish anything, that I wasn't worth the time investment, that I would never heal, that my grief would forever weigh me down. If I could beat the harness, I could beat my grief. And I felt like I was winning that battle session by session.

32

Worlds Apart

On February 7, I competed in a small interschool tournament at Seattle Gracie. That became the official weigh-in from which I measured my weight loss. I was 207, and there were no women in my weight class, so I had to roll with a guy—talk about giving me a complex. In BJJ, the weight classes for women are not very select. I'm in a group that is 162 pounds and over. Even at 207, I was fairly well-proportioned—I get big all over, I guess. Many of the women I competed against were short and round. Although I was four pounds heavier than I was at FemSport three months after Carly died, I was much leaner.

All the magazines say, "It's not about the number," but in reality it *is* about the number for some sports. And while it was not about the number in college volleyball, having your weight and body fat percentage posted in the locker room every Monday was enough to make you consider an eating disorder. I could not let weight loss be my goal for Worlds. And why would I? My weight class did not require that I cut weight.

But the weight did come off. I didn't even think about it, but the changes to my diet and the consistent interval training must have kicked my metabolism into a previously dormant gear. By the tournament time, I had lost almost twenty pounds. Twenty fewer pounds and beet juice? My endurance was great. I could move more quickly and more easily. I actually felt like an athlete again.

Kathleen continued to be my mental health coach. We talked about mental-endurance techniques I could use to make it through the dreaded month of April, and then carry on into June and the tournament. I told Kathleen about how nervous I would get before competition. I couldn't sleep because takedowns and sweeps would play over and over in my head. Other times, I would wake in the middle of the night, sweaty and choking my pillow. The day of the competition I wouldn't be able to eat because I feared I would throw up. I didn't want to take these antics with me to Worlds, so we created a mix of relaxation dialogue for my iPod.

The mental-strength process was very introspective. Kathleen asked me to identify three succinct goals for the competitive process. One was a training goal that would take me into the tournament. The second was a goal during the tournament. The third was my goal for two weeks after the tournament. The first two were easy to identify. While training, I wanted to be calm and confident. I wanted my energy to be clear and focused on the task at hand, and I wanted the anticipation to be exciting. During the tournament, I wanted to be fully present, calm, quick, and confident, knowing what to do. I wanted to keep moving, breathe, find the flow, and "make the second effort," as the coaches had encouraged. Kathleen rephrased everything into 'I will" statements with visualization cues.

It was the third goal that I had never considered. I was familiar with the idea of goal-setting in sports, but I had never been asked what I wanted to get out of a contest two weeks after it was over. I thought about this goal for quite some time before I answered. I wanted to feel positive about the experience. I wanted an increased sense of camaraderie. I wanted to be proud of my courage and accomplishment, and I wanted to embrace life again.

I listened to my iPod, I took a plane, and I went to the tournament on June 1. Several pages could be written about the tournament experience, but I'll condense it for the sake of focus, despite that there are a couple of good stories to tell. It was exciting to be part of an international tournament with teams from Mongolia, Sweden, China, Japan, and, of course, Brazil. The intensity with which the Brazilians cheered for their competitors was inspiring; it was obvious that Jiu-Jitsu is much more of a mainstream sport in Brazil than in the United States.

The gym floor was covered with mats for a total of ten rings. There was Jiu-Jitsu going on all day every day. I thought I would have my fill of BJJ, but it never got old. There was so much to see and learn that I didn't know about, but there was also a lot that I did know: moves I recognized, mistakes that I might make myself. It was a remarkable observation, which validated for me that I had every right to be there.

It's quite an ordeal to check in, get your gi checked, find your ring, and stay calm. My check-in was a debacle. No one had heard my name called so when I finally checked in on my check-in, my ring leader already had my name scratched. So we got that cleared up, and then I almost got disqualified because I couldn't get my wedding ring off. I had always worn it in local tournaments, and no one had ever said anything. I yanked on it hard, held my hand in the air, spit on it, twisted it—as my eyes teared up with panicked humiliation. I finally got it off, but not without a huge blister on the side of my swollen finger. I couldn't get my ring back on for five days afterward. Yeah, nice and calm. No problem. I'm a rock (not).

I had my match. It went okay. I blew my takedown by going in too straight and not putting my head in the right place, which led me to take myself down in the end. And then I was on the bottom, under my nemesis body type: "short-round." I hung in there, but I had taken myself down with only forty-five seconds left and just never recovered. I'm sure my coaches could say more. I haven't wanted to watch the tape. I'm sure I look like a bug being squished under a large, stubby thumb.

When I texted everyone who wanted to know, I just told them, "I lost, but I'm not a loser."

After my match was over, I shook hands with "short-round," pinched myself to make sure I was still awake and walked to the side where Coach was waiting. I did not feel too terribly disappointed. I did have some grappler's remorse . . . *if only I had* . . . and I was babbling with nervous energy. Coach was nodding and then he said, "Well, next time you—"

My head snapped up to look him in the eye. "Aren't I done? Can't I be done?"

Somewhere in my grandiose plan, I'm sure it was written that if I trained hard and stepped onto The Big Stage, then I could be done. I wouldn't ever have to compete again or train that hard (or drink beet juice). But Coach was shaking his head, "No, you're not done."

And being the young, wise sage that he is, he was right. I wasn't done.

And I'm still not done. Will any of us ever really be done? Where would I go if I was done? What would I do? What could possibly be more rewarding than what I had been a part of for the last five months? I was part of a process that transformed me into a better human being.

And the journey continues, does it not? If we stop chasing goals and pushing ourselves, and if we just settle, then we will stop growing and never realize the potential we have to live fully.

Yup, Coach was right. I'm most certainly not done.

33

World's Greatest Food Stories

My trip to the World Championships in Long Beach, California, was the first time I traveled to a tournament as an adult member of a team and not as the coach or as the chaperone of teenagers. It was apparent that being an adult team member means that you are treated, well, like an adult. "Everyone just kinda does their own thing," was what I heard when I inquired about flights, hotel arrangements, and rental cars. *Hmmm, there wasn't a team mom doing all of this for us?* I had to be my own team mom and worry only about myself. That thought was both liberating and lamentable.

Our small but mighty team consisted of myself (novice division/ white belt), Rich (white belt in the area for a wedding so why not roll), Ken "Rhino" (blue belt), Ethan "E-Dub" (purple belt), Bingo (brown belt), and Coach. The order of events called for the white belts to roll on the first day, the blue belts the next day, and then purple belts and so on. Team Foster had someone competing each day.

I arrived the day before the competition started and met some of the team at the hotel. We were going to drive to Irvine to work out at the gym of Coach's coach, the esteemed BJJ practitioner and professional MMA fighter, Giva "The Arm Collector" Santana (so named because he has won thirteen of his seventeen professional MMA bouts by armbar). Giva's gym was in full swing, and we took a corner of the mat to loosen up and roll lightly. It was a privilege to watch Coach roll with his mentor, one of the best in BJJ. After hugs, "thank yous," and "see you at the tourney," we took off for the first of several laughable tales that revolved around food.

Well, at least I found them laughable, because I was the only one on the team not cutting weight. I wasn't even required to weigh in for my division (162 pounds and above). The gentlemen, on the other hand, would be disqualified for being even one-tenth of a pound over at weigh-ins. E-Dub had to lose fifteen pounds before his match and he started the process two weeks before Worlds. Rhino and Bingo each had to lose twelve pounds and brought sauna suits in their carry-ons. Why we went to eat at a Mexican restaurant, I will never understand. If I had to sit across from a bottomless bowl of chips and not touch them, you would have had to duct tape my arms to the chair. Coach and I ordered whatever we wanted off the menu and munched on chips, while the guys had taco salad without the meat, tortilla shell, cheese, sour cream, or guacamole, and washed it down with southern California water that tasted mildly of wading pool.

The next day, I rolled.

On the second day of the tournament, Rhino rolled, so he was thereafter released from the bondage of caloric deprivation and got to pick where we ate lunch. We ended up at Boston Market. What transpired was a restaurant endorsement debacle. Rhino was starving, so he ordered the first appetizer on the menu. The waitress disappears, returns, and says that they are out of those . . . "How about the mozzarella sticks? They're my favorite." Sure, okay, bring some mozzarella sticks. Waitress disappears, returns, and says, "Oops, we don't even have mozzarella sticks (giggle giggle). Oh, I . . . uh . . . just, like, had them when I went out last night and (giggle giggle) that must have been what I was thinking."

Who wouldn't have been flustered standing in front of a cloud of testosterone and four sets of shoulders so wide I was forced to balance on one butt cheek from the edge of the booth?

After that, they failed to have what I wanted to order, and I learned that Coach is very serious about his food. He wouldn't let me have one yam fry off his plate. He made me order my own. I felt like the little boy who didn't get a star. Every calorie is precious if you want to keep your guns loaded, I guess. The last insult to our consumer satisfaction came when Bingo, with two and a half more days to cut weight, got a bill for three dollars because he ate five celery sticks.

That night, we ate California Pizza Kitchen so that E-Dub and Bingo could order whole-wheat–crusted pizza without cheese or meat and some plain lettuce. E-Dub, looking like a poster child for malnourishment, was mesmerized by the table placard displaying the seasonal dessert: mile-high strawberry shortcake with whipped cream.

"After tomorrow (drool) that's what I'm gonna get. We hafta come back here." Okay, E-Dub, you bet. Meanwhile, Bingo was shell-shocked that his bill included an additional four-dollar charge because he indulged in a couple of tomato slices.

E-Dub rolled the next morning, and we spent the day at the expo center watching some high-caliber competitions. As promised, we hit up California Kitchen Pizza again so E-Dub could have his mile-high shortcake. Unfortunately for E-Dub, his stomach had shrunken so much it couldn't manage the whole mile. It was more like a couple of blocks and some whip. Bingo became the replacement poster child, drooling over the same placard.

Friday night was the day before my birthday, so the guys took me to a movie and for a lesson. If am capable of learning anything at all in this life, it is this: when you are the only person in a group who has not seen all of the movies that preceded the movie you are watching, you must not ask any questions about the movie plot or characters. To do so puts you not only at risk of being ostracized, but when done in a group of Jiu-Jitsu–practicing males, can lead to serious bodily harm. The movie of note? "X-Men: First Class."

At this point, Bingo was the only one left to roll. Or what was left of Bingo to roll. We then headed back to California Pizza Kitchen for his mile-high. But, in what would turn out to be the biggest disappointment of the trip, they were out of strawberry shortcake. Bingo, his lust for shortcake rebuffed, receives a few bro-hugs from the guys, pulls himself together, and says, "That's okay, I want In-N-Out Burger." So off we went.

The anticipation during the ride was like waiting for manna from heaven. Manna? We found Mecca: right next-door to In-N-Out Burger was a Chick-Fil-A! We had reached nirvana . . . or at least the men had. I was coming off five months of beet juice and a nutritional overhaul. I wasn't sure I could digest a burger without seeing it twice.

The guys looked like hyenas over a kill—heads bowed, jaws grinding, traces of ketchup in the corners of their mouths, runaway lettuce on their shirts, an errant French fry making its escape under the table. It was an Animal Planet episode right there in the In-N-Out parking lot. I watched, transfixed, my Tiny Tot burger getting cold in its red plastic basket. This display was indeed evidence that the metabolism and gastroenterologic tolerance of the male stomach supersedes that of the average female.

Before Worlds, I had set my goals with Kathleen. I wanted to feel positive about the experience—even two weeks or more after worlds. I wanted an increased sense of camaraderie. I wanted to be proud of my courage and accomplishment, and I wanted to embrace life again. It was now three days since I competed, and I felt I was well on my way to achieving this goal. I had engaged fully in a novel undertaking that left me feeling positive about the sport of BJJ and competition. I had shared that experience with teammates who were now friends. I was proud of myself. I had followed through. I felt happier, more lighthearted, and I knew that the outlook from which I had previously viewed my life would never be the same.

34

No What-ifs

Coach has called me Doubting Thomas on more than one occasion. Although I have trained hard, studied the art, gone to seminars, and taken lessons, I have a tendency to question myself. I considered myself fairly confident before Carly died. I believed I could do anything. I had accomplished most everything I set out to do—athletically, academically, professionally, and personally. And then my life changed abruptly and painfully, and I stopped believing I was that capable anymore.

One of the most painful insecurities of my grief is that I have not had any dreams about Carly. Other people have dreams of her. They tell them to me, and I love to hear these stories. They make me smile . . . and they make me grimace with envy. I torture myself to tears with the intimation of not having my own Carly dreams. I ask myself:

What if there is no truth to spirits and souls?

What if my subconscious is protecting me because I won't be able handle the dreams, because I'm still afraid?

What if I open my heart and get hurt again?

What if I never find peace beneath my suffering?

What if the fact that I'm not dreaming of her means I'm forgetting her?

What if I have grieved wrongly, not loved enough?

What if I'm not good enough to be loved, to heal, to continue to grow and nurture others, and allow the same for myself?

What if I am too weak to move my pain?

I conversely have stretches of time when I am ruminating over exciting things I have been doing or are planning to do and my mind automatically goes to thinking, "I can't wait to tell Carly about this" and "Carly will love this idea." During those moments, I feel her presence so absolutely clearly, so honestly, and so intensely that I feel at peace—a sense of calm washes over me and I know I am in a place that is good, powerful, and whole. I don't want it to end.

Then I hit the wall, when my reverie is interrupted by the other side of my brain that reminds me that she is gone, that I won't be telling her these things or hearing her laugh, asking to join me, and then starting to make plans. Those intrusive thoughts stop me midstride. I yearn to go back to that peaceful place I was in just seconds ago. I want to make those moments last longer. Those are the moments when I know completely that she is with me.

One morning, I checked my phone and found a message from Carly's friend Morganne. Apparently she and another friend, Cody, both had a similar dream that night, and Morganne wanted to tell me about it (via text, of course: teenagers!). In the dream, the girls were hanging out at teammate's house. The girls were talking together when Carly walked into the room. They all looked up in surprise, which then turned into crying and hugging. They were so happy to see her. At one point during the reunion, Morganne asked Carly, "Are you going to see your mom, go say hi?" And Carly looked at her, shrugged it off, and replied with a *don't be silly* tone, "No, I'm with her all the time." Implying, that she's knows I'm all right and that I could wait . . . and like many teenagers, that she wanted to spend some time with her friends. Morganne sensed that Carly was checking in on them first because they were so young and confused, and she wanted them to know that she was okay, that it—what happened, the whole of the event, everything—was okay.

Of course I cried when I read this message from Morganne. I felt that nagging bitter emotional reflux coming up into my throat, "Why can't I have my own dream?"

I think about those feelings now—now that I am honing my acceptance skills with the idea that there are no what-ifs—and the doubt dissipates.

I don't have dreams about her because I don't need to dream of her; she is always with me.

———

Coach wants us to roll with confidence, and with that, he preaches about how there are no what-ifs. Although he teaches us everything we need to know about a particular technique, it's unrealistic to think that he can teach us every possible reaction to every action. Only we can relieve ourselves of doubt and trust that we'll know the right thing to do. When Coach is teaching, he explains to us why we make certain small movements, why a hand placement or a specific grip is necessary. The large movements are easy to see. It is the small details that are hard to see. It is from within us the self-confidence allows us to succeed at the small details, and that's what Coach encourages us to remember.

I have noticed when I am rolling well in a sparring situation, when I have the upper hand, that some opponents will start to verbally correct my moves. Are they asking themselves at that moment, "What if I can't beat a girl?" Fearing emasculation, they want to show me they are more knowledgeable and more skilled than I. Their own self-doubt fosters a blemish of denial that I might just kick their ass, so they had better save their pride.

Coach knows our various levels of skill and gives us appropriate tactics so that we feel equipped to compete. He points out that certain moves work best with certain body types, but that we should not feel limited. Every body type is different. We differ in flexibility, length, center of gravity, strength, and balance, so we must take the tools provided and make them work for us. He has reasonable levels of expectation for each of us. He just won't accept "what if."

> *"Our doubts are traitors and make us*
> *lose the good we oft might win,*
> *by fearing to attempt."*
>
> — William Shakespeare

There is no room in a competitive mind for doubt. When I entered my first competition nine months after I started at Foster, I had little idea what I was doing. There were no what-ifs for me at that time because I did not know what to expect; I just stepped on the mat, albeit as nervous as wrinkle on Dolly Parton, and competed. I started with the leg reap takedown and moved to side control. I passed her guard. I even remembered to breathe once or twice. And I won that very first match. I didn't question what I was doing, I just did it.

Unfortunately, it was downhill from there because as I learned and became more acquainted with the skills I was up against, I did start questioning myself. For example, after that first match my next opponent was bigger than me: "What if she's stronger than me?" "What if I don't do as well as last time?" "What if I mess up?" There was doubt all-up-in-my-head. And I have lost every match since then whenever my opponent is bigger than me. I continue to work on this.

Coach is proud every time any of us just step onto the mat. He reminds us that "you learn more from a loss than from a win." I think I'm missing something.

———

On Carly's last day with me, she was wearing a shirt that said "The world is pretty amazing."

Carly's path did not include "what-ifs."

There are no what-ifs is that last bastion of living life to the fullest. Carly participated in and accomplished a great many things in fifteen years. Some people tell me she did this because she knew her time on Earth was short. I don't think so. That philosophy implies that she wouldn't have done all of those things if she didn't need to, if she knew she had lots of time. Carly saw the world as a truly awesome place, with exciting people to meet and wondrous places to go, with inspiring music to hear and play, with rousing games to play, and with exquisite gifts of life to share.

And because she saw the world this way, she lived without what-ifs. She lived each day fully, curious and willing. She found ways to see the positive in her experiences and move beyond setbacks and uncertainty.

She continues to teach me lessons with how she lived: that I should embrace each day as the gift it is, not because it's a stepping stone to something better.

> *"When I let go of what I am,*
> *I become what I might be."*
>
> — Lao Tzu

35

Elena Anew

The last four years have been an emotional collage of sadness, joy, anger, hope, doubt, belief, callousness, trust, struggle, and triumph.

It has been a journey to find out who I was without my daughter. The topography of my journey has brought me from the lowest of lows, across chasms of self-doubt, back and forth on switchbacks of progress toward goals that resided at seemingly unreachable elevations.

It has been a journey to find out if I mattered. I did not know my worth.

It has been a journey to redefine myself as a person who survived a tragic event and came out the other side whole.

I have people in my life who have known me since I was young, people I know from my choice to live in Washington, people I know because of Carly, and people I know who did not know Carly or me as Carly's mom. Each has been an observer and a participant, and each has played that incomparable role of assisting me along the way.

I struggled to find a new sense of balance. My family would never be the same, and so I needed to recalibrate the scales. That is hard to do with a cloud of guilt stifling you. I wore my lack of balance on my sleeve.

I remember being stopped before stepping on the mat and told to take some deep breaths. I was told that, when I stepped on the mat, I had to let everything go and be present. Training was to be a mental sanctuary, a place to clear your mind and relieve yourself of burdens.

I have not mastered this tactic, but over time, I have gotten better at it. Sometimes I would be trying to clear my mind, only to have my issues move closer to the surface. Once, I had gone to practice stressed over some inner turmoil. I had participated, but became increasingly distracted by what I was trying to let go of. The more I told myself to stop thinking about it, the more I thought about it. I was in lineup when I knew I just wasn't going to be able to keep it together, so I asked if I could leave. I went in the lobby and started to take off my gi. I had meant leave, as in go home, but that was not what Coach had in mind.

Coach entered the lobby and told me I couldn't leave—that if I left, I gave all the power to what was bothering me. He told me to calm myself down and return to the gym. I didn't have to roll anymore, but I had to stay. In a deeper way, he meant "stay the course."

Stay the course. I would not have achieved the balance I sought if I had run away from the very place that got me on course. At the gym, I found a place where I could trust myself and others. A place where it was safe to fall apart because I knew someone would help me put myself back together. A place that would challenge me physically, mentally, and spiritually.

When I had first stepped into Foster Brazilian Jiu-Jitsu, I did not know that not only would I recover my sense of who I was, but I would also find myself far more capable than I ever gave myself credit for. I could achieve in spite of my grief. Even though I lost my daughter, I didn't have to lose myself. I did not want to grieve her anymore; I did not wish to be lost. In finding myself, I can show Carly how deeply I love her.

> *"You may never know what results come of your action, but if you do nothing there will be no result."*
>
> — Mahatma Gandhi

How is a journey measured when its beginning is the only definitive point a person has? Is it measured by the time that has passed? By some tangible effect: the prize, the job, the finish line? I had no choice but to embark on this journey. I didn't want to be on it, but I was. I had no goal in my crosshairs. But I did have trust. Trust in my family, friends, Coach, and Jiu-Jitsu; trust that strengthened me to ride out difficult times. It nurtured courage and promise, and over time I knew it was leading me in the right direction. My promotion to blue belt was not my goal, but when Coach tied that belt around my waist, I knew that my journey was a worthy one. And when he took my white belt and tied it in a tight knot so that it could not be worn again, I finally had a measure of my journey. My most difficult days and my struggles to simply survive were behind me, and I could not go back there again.

I now have an answer to Susan's question: Is it good for my soul? Jiu-Jitsu gave me back my soul.

On June 17th, 2011, I was promoted to a blue belt in Jiu-Jitsu.

I got my blue belt! (photo by Mike Baltierra).

*"Perhaps strength doesn't reside
in having never been broken,
but in the courage required
to grow strong in the broken places."*

— Anonymous

Glossary of Brazilian Jiu-Jitsu Common Terminology

Armbar—An armbar is a type of submission that results in hyperextending an opponent's arm. There are many ways to obtain an armbar, but the finish is similar:
1. Your elbow is controlled.
2. Your hips are tight against your opponent's armpit.
3. Your opponent's wrist is kept vertical with the thumb pointed upward.
4. Your opponent's arm is squeezed between your knees.
5. As your opponent's arm is extended, your hips are thrust forward, putting pressure on their elbow joint.

Frame—Framing is when you use arms, legs, knees, or hands to create and maintain space between you and your opponent. Framing is not pushing; it is creating a barrier.

Gi—A lightweight, two-piece, usually white garment worn by barefooted martial-arts participants, consisting of loose-fitting pants and a wraparound jacket with cloth belt.

Guard—There are three main types of guard: closed guard, open guard, and half guard.
1. For the closed guard, your legs are used to control your opponent's torso by wrapping your legs around your opponent's waist and locking your ankles. This position allows for control from side to side, frontward, and backward, breaking your opponent's posture.
2. In open guard, the legs are used to control your opponent but are not closed around the opponent. This guard is more dynamic and involves using the feet to push, pull, and hook the opponent.

3. In the half guard, your opponent is halfway through passing your guard, and you have only one of your opponent's legs controlled. Although it may seem that this position provides less control, it is very useful to disrupt your opponent's center of gravity and set him up to be attacked or swept.

Hook—Hooks are when you use a foot or leg, or both, to control an opponent

Knee-on-belly—This move involves placing your knee or shin on an opponent's abdomen with the same foot off of the mat; your other leg is bent in a lunging position by your opponent's head, but out of reach of his arm. Your grips are usually on one of your opponent's sleeves and his pants, and your opponent is bearing most of your weight. Knee-on-belly is often used to secure an opponent before transitioning.

Lineup—The lineup is the starting and ending stance taken by all training participants, done from right to left with members of the highest rank on the right. A variation is to have multiple rows from front to back with the highest-ranking members in the front. The lineup precedes the act of bowing to your instructor.

Mount—A classic dominant position, the mount is where you sit on top of your opponent, who is bearing most of your weight. Your feet are alongside his or her hips or tucked under his or her thighs. High mount is when your weight is mostly on your opponent's chest and your knees are in his armpits, making use of the arms difficult. Low mount is where your weight is mostly on his or her abdomen. Regardless of high or low, being on the bottom makes you very vulnerable to attacks, and it is difficult to breathe.

Passing Guard—Passing guard is the dissolution of your opponent's guard, resulting in getting completely around both of his legs and attaining positional control.

Posting—When you post, you use an arm or leg to maintain balance while attacking or defending.

Roll—This is BJJ vernacular for going to the mat and grappling with another person. Common usage: "Hey, wanna roll?"

Shrimp—To shrimp, or elbow escape, is a key movement in many escapes from the bottom and is used to make space. It must be combined with other elements to become an escape. The move is done from your side by raising your hips off of the mat, using your shoulder as the fulcrum, and thrusting the hips backwards. This brings your head closer to your feet, and if you froze the moment, you would look like a curled shrimp, head to tail.

Side Control—Side control is a secure way to hold your opponent and control his upper body. From the side, it looks like pinning him to the mat, using your bodyweight and grips. With good technique, you can rest for a moment here before transitioning to another position.

Submit—When you submit, you yield to the power or authority of another.

Submission—This is any technique used to cause someone to submit, or to tap. Chokes, armbars, leg locks, and triangles are common submission moves. In sport or competition Jiu-Jitsu, a submission results in a match win.

Sweep—A sweep is a swift and steady motion that results in your opponent ending up on his back from your guard.

Takedown—A takedown is a move or series of moves used to bring an opponent to the mat from a standing position. Many takedowns resemble Judo throws and include leg trips, arm drags, and controlling the head.

Tap—To tap, or tap out, is when a participant submits to his opponent. This is done by tapping your opponent on the closest body part or the mat with your hand or foot. If no appendage or mat is accessible, the submitee can call out "tap."

Triangle—Triangle is a submission technique that places your opponent's head between the thigh of one of your legs and the back of knee of your other leg. This is considered a "blood choke" because it restricts the blood flow to your opponent's brain, as opposed to cutting off his ability to breath.

Turtle—This position involves curling yourself up into a ball, hiding your elbows inside your knees, and protecting your neck—a defensive position that you generally do not want to find yourself in, but it is better than being pinned to the mat.

References

Inspirational quotations are identified throughout the novel. For those that are attributed to anonymous, all efforts were made to verify a source.

Saulo Ribeiro and Kevin Howell. *Jiu-Jitsu University*. Auberry, CA: Victory Bely Publishing, 2008.

Hickney, Matthew. *Walking to the Cage*. 2009. www.imdb.com/name/nm1680821. matthickney@hotmail.com.

Rollmates and Soulmates

Foster Brazilian Jiu-Jitsu
Address: 1256 S. 192nd Street, Kent, Washington 98032
Phone: 253.208.3270
Email: coach@fbjjonline.com
Website: www.fbjjonline.com/

Dr. Lisa Chavez
Good Natured Medicine
Address: 402 NE 72nd Street, Suite 3, Seattle, Washington 98115
Phone: 206.686.5012
Website: www.goodnaturedmedicine.com

Kathleen O'Connor, LMHC
Grief and Life Transitions
Address: 20042 19th Avenue NE, Lower Level, Shoreline, Washington 98155
Phone: 206.227.1826
Website: www.griefandlifetransitions.com

Dr. Steve Zografos
Kent Sport and Spine
Address: 24909 104th Ave SE, Suite 103, Kent, Washington 98030
Phone: 253.850.8163
Website: www.kentsportspine.com

Joanne Kovaly, PMA-CPT, LMP, MMLT
Website: www.bodyshoppepilates.com

Louise Anderson, LMP
Ashiatsu Massage
Website: www.deepfeet.com

And, of course, the website address for The Carly Stowell Foundation:
www.Carlystowellfoundation.org

In Retrospect and Thanks

Putting my journey through grief on paper was truly an exercise in self-rediscovery. The writing process, at first, was like staring into a reflecting pool and seeing all of the surrounding features, but never seeing me. It took time, patience, and great effort before I began to see myself in the pool. There were periods of hypnotic rippling and soothing calm. My writing reflected my journey right back at me. It made me look and finally see myself amongst the familiar features that never strayed from my frame of view. The honesty of the reflection told me that my life and my family would never be the same and that I would never be the same, but that I still fit into the world I saw in the pool.

Lifesavers, All Flavors

I have many familiar faces to thank for staying in my frame of view and for keeping me in theirs:

Chuck for his endearing looks of wonder and amazement and reminders to jog, not sprint, through life;

For my sons, **Eason and Carson**, who miss their sister and had to miss me for a while, thanks for waiting;

My parents, **Bruce and Rita**, and my brothers **Mark and Alan (and their families)**, for walking this walk with me since the beginning;

The **Clans O'Brien and the Seattle and Portland Clans**;

Susan, who asked the right question;

Doc C who first taught me about courage;

Christine, Kelly, Carrie, Selena, Dianna, Lorri, Jen, and Mary, my gal pals who drove me places, planted flowers in my yard, and pried me off the floor;

Cody, KTB, Kendall, Jaclyn, Kylie, Morganne, Chanel, Jill, "P," Tyler, Cynthiann, Ashlyn, Riley, Carly's friends who never let me forget that they remember;

Carly's music guides, **Dee and Doug**;

Carly's coaches who guided her toward her basketball dream, **Scott, Kaas, Phil, Mike,** and especially **Mo Hines,** who taught her to train with purpose and play with passion;

And our special family friends, many of whom share their time, love, and knowledge through the Carly Stowell Foundation: **Dave and Diane, Quentin, Debbie and Alan, Lorri and Rick, Ron and Eileen, Jim, Joyce, Jenny and Brent, Laurie, Loreli, EZ, and Second Wind.**

It goes without saying that I owe a great deal of my healing to **Team Foster**:

Coach James, whose words make a difference and whose contributions are more valuable than he may think, and his wife **Amy,** who so generously shares him with us;

Big Rick, who still makes sure my glass is always half full;

Coaches Bill, ToDD, Jeff H, Jeff B, Bingo, Thad, Bobi, Trevin, Jimmie, Mark, and everybody that I have swapped sweat with on the mat. Some of you are extra special, I hope you know who you are.

Much gratitude for my mental and physical health also goes to my **Wellness Team**:

Kathleen, my listener who always has tissue;

Lisa, who first suggested I write down my stories;

And **JoAnn, Doctor Z, Louise, Dr. Feeney**.

And thank you to my newest but no less important friends: **Jan** (www. thewordverve.com), editor extraordinaire who read my manuscript and from the very first "wow" enveloped me with her positive energy, encouragement, and sentence restructuring; and **Terri, Katy, and Julie**, my publishing team at BQB.

Finally (for now), I give thanks to two other daughter-spirits who are in my heart, **Ashley and Rebekah**.